Know-How on the Job:
The Important Working Knowledge of "Unskilled" Workers

Westview Replica Editions

Know-How on the Job:
The Important Working Knowledge
of "Unskilled" Workers

Ken C. Kusterer

Today's "unskilled" workers must acquire a substantial body
of knowledge to survive and succeed on their jobs--despite
mechanization and automation, despite bureaucratization and the
ever narrower division of labor, and despite Taylorist indus-
rial engineering. This working knowledge is indispensable to
the production process, yet it is informally learned and generally unrecognized by anyone outside the workplace. Acting together through communal networks, workers are able to use their
knowledge to carry on an informal "craft administration" for the
production of useful goods and services--an administration that
underlies, and in fact is presupposed by, management's "bureaucratic administration" directed toward control of costs and
production profits.

The unacknowledged existence of these valuable skills and
functions among supposedly unskilled workers helps to explain
why the experience of alienation is a more complex and contradictory phenomenon than theorists have expected. Alienated from
management and its cost-minimizing, profit-maximizing goals,
yet committed somehow to the workplace community and its goals
of use-value production, the consciousness of these workers en-
compasses contradictory elements, causing a fundamental ambivalence toward their work situation and their own work activity.

The author derives these conclusions from in-depth case
studies conducted in a bank and a paper products factory and
from interviews with a variety of workers in other blue- and
white-collar work situations. Most of the participating workers
were women, since they are disproportionately represented in
the lowest-paid and reputedly least-skilled jobs investigated
in this study.

Ken C. Kusterer holds degrees from Yale and Washington uni-
versities and is presently an associate professor at The
American University in Washington, D.C.

Know-How on the Job:
The Important Working Knowledge of "Unskilled" Workers

Ken C. Kusterer

A Westview Replica Edition

Copyright © 1978 by Westview Press, Inc.

Published in 1978 in the United States of America by
    Westview Press, Inc.
    5500 Central Avenue
    Boulder, Colorado 80301
    Frederick A. Praeger, Publisher

Library of Congress Catalog Card Number: 78-19632
ISBN: 0-89158-260-6

Printed and bound in the United States of America

To my family, to Faith and Jed and
Todd. For four years my obsession with
this project has dominated our family life.
Like a malignant growth, "Daddy's work"
has permeated every aspect of our relationships, taking over our vacations and
wrecking our weekends. It seems almost a
mockery to dedicate this, the cause of
such pain, to you. But in this case, love
means having to say it, in public print --
I am sorry.

Contents

PART II
WORKING KNOWLEDGE ANALYZED

Acknowledgements

Although I alone am responsible for its content, this work has benefited from the intellectual
work of many others, most importantly my informants
in the work places who contributed their own understandings and interpretations of the processes they
described for me. Many risked their jobs to participate in this study, and I am grateful to them all.
Thanks are also due to Ms. Dorothy Garrett and
Ms. Pat Redfern, whose work on this project has
demonstrated to me the depth of their working knowledge, both the "basic working knowledge" necessary
to type quality manuscripts and the "supplementary
working knowledge" necessary to handle problem
writers.
Over the years that I have been working on
this, a network of friends and colleagues, teachers
and students, past and present, has nourished and
nudged me along the way. Dennis Brunn, Robert
Boguslaw, Wolf Heydebrand, Jerry Grzyb, Irving
Zeitlin, Pedro Cavalcanti (especially Pedro), Adam
Przeworski, Alfonso Arrau, Muriel Cantor, Dave
Hakken, Paul Goldman, Richard Ratcliffe, Sam Fried-
man, Jan Houbolt, Dan Hoeschen, Dee Wernette,
Michael Yarrow, Samih Farsoun, Roberta Goldberg,
Phil Kraft, Sue Donahue, Bob Byington, Bob Porter,
Shirley Askew, Rob Burlage, Evan Stark, Steve Rose:
thank you all.
Members of one school of thought have had an
overwhelming influence on the perspective that informs this work, yet their work somehow is not cited
anywhere. I have so assimilated their world-view
that the bibliography, I am chagrined to discover,
does not even mention the many works of the people
I think of as the Detroit school -- Marty Glaberman,
Jim Rinehart, Seymour Faber, and especially my long-
time friend and mentor, George Rawick. To you all,
thanks too.

1. Introduction to the Perspectives, Methods, and Ethics of the Research

The original insight that led me to do this study was an extension and generalization of T.S. Kuhn's concept of the scientific paradigm (Kuhn, 1970a, 1970b, 1971). I had worked both as a printer and as a social scientist, and the two occupations seemed similar enough to suggest that the knowledge applied at work by the printer was of the same basic type as the knowledge of the scientist. It seemed possible to speak of workers' paradigms as well as scientists' paradigms. In the practice of their trade, printers seemed to function as rational, problem-solving, knowledge-acquiring "normal scientists," working out of an established knowledge base or paradigm, and constantly pushing at the frontiers of this paradigm as they encountered new situations and solved new problems.

Numerous conversations with friends who held "unskilled" jobs led to the further hunch that knowledge paradigms existed on every job, not just among scientists and skilled workers.

Following up this original insight led to the beginning stage in the development of the research, one which we might now in retrospect label the pilot study phase. This involved two different activities. On the one hand, I began to pick the brains of my friends in various jobs, in effect interviewing them about their work in the course of our discussions and conversations. On the other hand, I began to read more intensely in various contemporary theories of the sociology of knowledge, especially the neo-phenomenological writings of Peter Berger et al (1967, 1974) and Burkhardt Holzner (1972).

I was convinced that the subject of working knowledge was important, because I strongly believed in certain assumptions about the nature of society in general, and our society in particular, assump-

1

tions that are fairly common among sociologists, although all these assumptions are perhaps seldom combined in the same individual. These domain assumptions, about the effect of our social relations on our social consciousness, about the centrality of work in our lives, about the primacy of our economy in setting the limits of our societal choices -- all of these assumptions underpin this research, shaping its design and reconfirming themselves in its results. Gouldner (1970) and many other sociologists have stressed the central role of such assumptions in all scientific work, and have urged that social scientists become self-consciously reflective about them. Social science audiences should be forth-rightly informed of these assumptions, so they can better assess the utility and validity of the work. Toward that end, some small description of these assumptions of mine is necessary.

I accept the central tenet of both Marxist and phenomenological thought that the meaning statements and reality definitions which people develop out of their work experience form the most basic, most central level of knowledge, upon which all other consciousness is built. This is because work is the most basic level of praxis, the one sphere of human activity in which the worker is constantly seeing his reality definitions of the work situation tested and confirmed at first hand in the concrete results of his work activity. The world of work is the "most real" of all social life worlds. It is also the most "here and now" of bodily experiences:

> The reality of everyday life is organized around the "here" of my body and the "now" of my present.... This means that I exper-ience everyday life in terms of different degrees of closeness and remoteness, both spatially and temporally. Closest to me is the zone of everyday life that is directly accessible to my bodily manipu-lation. This zone contains the world within my reach, the world within which I act so as to modify its reality, or the world in which I work. (Berger and Luckmann, 1967, 22)

It follows, then, that the study of working knowledge is crucially important to any understand-ing of either work processes or consciousness for-mation. The study of working knowledge therefore has the potential of making a contribution to our

2

understanding of "class consciousness," that is, the consciousness of people who share similar work experiences because of similar positions in the relations of production. This is a central problem area in Marxist social science, one of historical materialism's weakest links.

One problem has been that most Marxist writing on the development of the working class has focused upon the political arena of overt conflict between workers and capitalists. Marxist scholars have studied working class movements, trade unions, political parties. They have tended to neglect the continuing basic "historical act" of the working class -- production.

Marxist scholars have specialized in searching for indicators that the working class is throwing off its false consciousness, growing increasingly militant, moving from a class "in itself" to a class "for itself." Yet they have too often confined this search to the superstructural levels of political activity and ideological belief. By their own theory, they should be watching intently developments in the evolution of relations of production. This is where the explanations of working class consciousness and political practice must be sought.

The working class develops not only through its struggle with capital, but also through changes in the basic common experience of the members of that class, their participation in production. For Marxists then, the core of the study of history is the study of work activity and work experience.

> We must begin by stating the first premise of all human existence and, therefore, of all history, the premise, namely, that men must be in a position to live in order to be able to 'make history'. But life involves before everything else eating and drinking, a habitation, clothing and many other things. The first historical act is thus the production of the means to satisfy these needs, the production of material life itself. And indeed this is an historical act, a fundamental condition of all history, which today, as thousands of years ago, must daily and hourly be fulfilled merely in order to sustain human life.... Therefore in any interpretation of history one has first of all to observe this fundamental fact in all of its significance and

3

all its implications and to accord its due
importance. (Marx, 1964 edition of 1847
original, 119-120)

Social science studies of work have experienced
an exhilarating resurgence in the 1970's, after at
least a decade of relative stagnation. The source
of this resurgence is probably the new rediscovery
and wide publicizing of militant dissatisfactions
of large segments of the labor force. The series of
strikes by highly paid auto workers dissatisfied
over working conditions in the General Motors plant
in Lordstown, Ohio was the catalyst for renewed concern over work, and the HEW Task Force Report, Work
in America, legitimized the workers' complaints.
The present form of work organization was again defined as a "social problem."*

In all this new wave of social policy analysts'
and social scientists' concern, the issues of control and alienation have become central, because
critical social scientists have followed the lead
of critical workers to make them central.

Illuminating the working knowledge of workers,
this study makes possible improved understanding of
both alienation and control. The sociological
theory of alienation is in sad shape after years of
stagnation since the work of Blauner (1964).
Blauner's work itself had serious problems. As a
result of his research in the textile industry, he
concluded that textile workers ought to be alienated. But they were not. He was forced to "explain"
this anomaly by reference to the work force being
composed of (1) woman and (2) small-town residents,
two social categories whose "social aspirations"
were so low that they didn't know enough to be
alienated (1964, 80). At present, the sociological
theory of alienation is so abstracted from reality
that Ritzer can write, and apparently believe:

> ...the assembly-line worker finds
> his job meaningless. He is unable to see
> what his very specialized task has to do
> with the work of others on the line.
> (1975, 224)

As Watson (1971), Swados (1958), and other former
auto workers have repeatedly pointed out, it is

---

*In fact, the Society for the Study of Social Problems
(SSSP) organized a Labor Studies Section in 1975.

4

exactly the transparent interdependency of work on the line that makes it so easy for auto workers to feel and show solidarity in such actions as wildcat strikes.

The study of authority and control in the workplace can also be advanced by a correct understanding of the role of working knowledge. All the current debates over experiments and reforms in workers' participation and workers' control could be improved by an analysis of exactly how much control workers now have, and how their exercise of it is either facilitated or limited by factors on the job that also affect working knowledge.

The Original Research Design

Motivated by these concerns, and acting out of basic assumptions about the centrality of the subject, I decided in 1974 to move my other, basically historical work onto the back burner, and to concentrate my research efforts on following up my hunch about the importance of working knowledge, even in "unskilled" jobs. The purposes of this research effort, as outlined in the original proposal, were to:

> build detailed ethnographic descriptions of (unskilled) work communities and their working knowledges; ...to demonstrate...the existence of this knowledge even on 'unskilled' jobs, the important contribution of this knowledge to productivity; (and to verify my) assumption that the sources and contents of particular bodies of working knowledge have important consequences for the quality of the life of the workers involved, affecting the type and degree of autonomy, alienation and satisfaction that they experience.

As is clear from these quotes taken out of the original proposal, although this was supposed to be an "exploratory" study, the "research questions" were not really questions at all, but assumptions and not-very-implicit hypotheses. The first step in the research process was therefore to elaborate this theory into a more explicit set of more testable assumptions and propositions. I attempted to do this by developing a theoretical synthesis that drew from various traditions, most importantly Marxist theories of work (Marx, 1967 edition of 1867

5

original; Watson, 1971; Stone, 1974; Marglin, 1974),* the more anthropological variants of American Industrial Sociology (principally Roy, 1952, 1954, 1960; Warner and Low, 1947; Whyte, 1948, 1961, 1969; and Gouldner, 1954, 1965), neo-Marxist and psychological theories of alienation (Seeman, 1959; Blauner, 1964; Israel, 1971), and the phenomenologically oriented sociology of knowledge (Schutz, 1962, 1964; Berger and Luckmann, 1970; Berger, Berger, and Kellner, 1974; and Holzner, 1972).

While I was developing this theory, I was also beginning to pre-test the interview schedule, and trying to gain access to a work situation. This last proved to be incredibly difficult. After months of trying, it appeared that the research would be halted right there. When I finally did get into the Cone Department, it was only under conditions that required considerable modification in the original data collection design. (See the discussion below under the heading of "Methods and Ethics: Confidentiality and Problems of Access.")

The sampling procedure that I attempted to follow in looking for appropriate work situations was a combination of a "worst case" strategy and an effort to assure that the cases would be reasonably "representative." The worst case strategy called for me to find the most apparently unskilled work that I could, in order to give my assumptions about the importance of working knowledge the severest possible test. Although it is stretching the point to refer to two case studies as a "representative sample," I at least wanted to ensure that the two work situations were as unlike each other as possible in all relevant aspects except that of the reputed level of skill. In particular I wanted to make sure that the two case studies represented: both blue collar and white collar work, different levels of technology (Blauner, 1964; Bright, 1971; Woodward, 1965), and different degrees of bureaucratization (Crozier, 1964; Blau, 1955; Gouldner, 1954). As it developed in the end, I was lucky to gain access to any work situations at all, and I had to take what I could get. Fortunately, the two work situations are quite different along most of these dimensions, although I would have preferred that the white collar situation be a larger, more

_____

*The most important recent contribution to this tradition (Braverman, 1974) had not yet been published.

6

bureaucratized department using a higher level of technology than was true in the branch bank.

Problems of Theory and Method: Reconceptualizing the Research Design

From the beginning, I knew that I would have to conduct an exploratory type of research. At first, the idea of an exploratory study implied for me a research design based on the use of case studies, the collection of qualitative data, and the combination of data collection methods which come naturally to field work -- my interpretation of the "methodological triangulation" of Webb et al (1966) and Denzin (1970). Unfortunately, these elements do not necessarily add up to an exploratory study. I had put together a research design that, although it emphasized qualitative data, was still essentially a modified form of a hypothesis-verification design.

My original proposed table of contents more or less tells the story: theory chapter, methods chapter, case studies chapters, conclusions. I was ambitious; the theory chapter was to be a real work of theoretical synthesis, not merely a "literature review." In the theory chapter I intended to use a time-honored critical method to review the work of a wide array of social theorists. This critical review would then serve as the basis for my own theoretical synthesis.

Four months of this study were spent reviewing these works and trying to put together a coherent theoretical system. Although at the time I was also pre-testing the first drafts of an interview schedule, I felt that it was vital that this theoretical synthesis be complete before I began research on the actual case studies. I felt the theory was necessary to guide the research, to tell me, since my time was limited, precisely what to look for, which questions to ask, and what data to collect. I fretted that circumstances forced me to begin my first case study before this theory chapter was finished. Clearly, although I was intending to use "soft" methods, I was approaching my research design from the standard hypothetical-deductivist perspective: first formulate the theory, then collect the data to verify it. Since this was to be an exploratory study, I never intended to formalize the theory into a system of strict hypotheses to be tested with the apparatus of inferential statistical techniques, but I did expect that the case studies would either confirm aspects of the theory or suggest ways in which it should be modified.

This theory-before-data perspective was giving me trouble from the beginning. I remember particularly the problem of the formal definition of the concept of "work community." This was a troublesome concept, first used in a very loose way by Watson (1971) and Valmeras (1971). I had taken their concept, merged it with Holzner's "epistemic community," reshaped it in accordance with my understanding of the whole Gemeinschaft and community studies tradition in sociology. I had finally come up with a definition that I felt was clear and unambiguous, capable of withstanding rigorous logical criticism. Yet I knew at the time from the feedback I was getting in my pre-test interviews that there was something wrong with this concept. Pure and beautiful as it was in its formal definition, the work communities out there in the real world were not quite what the definition defined. The deductive logic suggested that I would have to discard the concept, but I couldn't -- it was a central pivot upon which the whole theoretical system hinged. I finally decided that the only way out of the dilemma was to just "hang loose," hoping that in the course of the case studies I would discover some analogous concept that would take the place of the work community in my theoretical structure.

This is of course exactly what happened. As soon as I stopped trying to shoe-horn my worker informants' statements into my work community category, the real social relations became obvious. There was no "work community," not even any of the "informal work groups" that traditional industrial sociology had made famous. The problem had been that I could not find any group boundaries, although informal work relations were clearly everywhere. Workers did not create for themselves a closed-bounded work community, but they did create a network or "grapevine" of communal relationships that bind each worker (more or less, allowing for individual personality differences) into relations of trust and solidarity ("cohesion") to the other workers that she interacts with in the course of her concrete work tasks.

In other words, there were no informal closed-bounded work groups, but there were informal networks. From the point of view of each individual worker, there was a finite group of "significant other" fellow workers, but each worker's "work

8

community" was slightly different, depending on her
location in the formal organization of production.
This network, although it is more nebulous than a
bounded work community would be, is also more functional for the workers, both as a mechanism for
craft administration and as a mechanism for workers'
collective self defense.

The lesson that I draw from this example is not
that if I had happened to have a background in
Sociometrics instead of in classical industrial
sociology then my a-priori theory would have been
more adequate, but that one is better off if one
allows the theory formulation to occur as a simul-
taneous, complementary process to the data collection rather than as a process that is already complete when the data collection begins. In other
words, methodologies of verification are not com-
patible with exploratory research.

By the end of the Cone Department study, the
gap between theory and data indicated that something
was clearly wrong with the plan of the research.
The problem was not that the data contradicted the
theory -- in small areas it did, but mostly it did
not. The problem was that most of the concepts and
categories in the theory had found no applicability
in the analysis of the case study, and many of the
most clear-cut concepts that had emerged from the
case study were not especially anticipated by the
theory. Believing that theory should be useful as
well as elegant, I decided to drop the theory, to
concentrate on the clarification and development of
the concepts arising out of the research, and to
consider picking up again those elements of the
theory that helped explain real questions arising
out of the research process.*

This decision greatly facilitated the rest of
the research. During the process of trying to
start up the data collection for a second case
study, I was exposed to several different work
situations. When I first tried to apply Glaser and
Strauss' method to this building collection of comparative data, I was rewarded immediately with a
rush of new insights which rapidly and almost
effortlessly flowered into definite conceptual
categories. The ease with which these new theo-

_____

*The principal influence that lead me to adopt this strat-
egy was Glaser and Strauss' "constant comparative method
of qualitative analysis" (1967, 105-113).

9

retical elements could be developed, and the relative enthusiasm which they generated when I tried them out on the informants, made a gratifying comparison with the difficulty of the speculative theory development that I had engaged in earlier.

As anybody who reads the body of the study can appreciate, I am not trying to claim that these theoretical elements "arose out of the data." What arose out of the data were certain previously ignored important phenomena that were in need of explanation. The theoretical insights that were eventually developed into the explanations came primarily from existing sociological work. At this stage of the research I was also teaching a survey course in classical sociological theory, an arrangement that I recommend highly to other researchers. As I was studying work situations and puzzling over some of the problems that they presented, the course was proceeding, survey-fashion, through some of the key works of the major theorists. Comte, Durkheim, Simmel, Weber, and especially Toennies -- the theory of each provided some little element that provided precisely the insight necessary to understand some puzzling aspect of these work situations.* This is how the process of "abduction" (Peirce, 1955; Hanson, 1958) works. Unlike either inductive or deductive research designs, the two tasks of theory generation and data collection must go on simultaneously. Each new theoretical insight must be checked out against data, and often the data that is needed has not been previously collected, because such data had not seemed important until the generation of this new insight. Conversely, as the data builds up and provides a wider basis for comparison, the theoretical categories need to be modified to account for the newly discovered variations.

As a result of this reconceptualization, not only the design but also the purpose of the research was subtley changed. By the last revision of the research proposal, the goal of the research was:

> To produce a body of grounded theory
> about: (a) the organizational structure
> of work organizations, which determines
> the development of (b) bodies of working

---

*Marx's name is not listed here only because this study owes its whole world-view, not just "little elements," to his theory.

knowledge, which in turn condition both
(c) organizational productivity and
(d) the alienation and autonomy of workers. All good scientific theory should
be useful to scientists in their further
research. But, unlike much theorizing in
social science, theory that is grounded
in empirical reality should be useful
also as a practical guide to the people
involved in the social situations that
the theory is about.... It is the
ambition of this research to create
concepts that will add as much to the
practical knowledge of workers as they
do to the practical knowledge of social
scientists.

Data Sources and Data Collection Techniques

The basic research role followed in this study
is that of the "observer as participant" (Gold,
1958). In none of these work situations did I
participate as a worker. Nor was I granted formal
access to any of them as an observer. The observations that were made were brief sessions, primarily
useful as a kind of orientation session necessary
for me to be able to follow what workers were saying
in their interviews. The observations occurred
early in the process of collecting data on each work
situation, and in each case only my initial informant was aware of the purpose of my visit to the
work place. For each visit to a work place, there
was a cover story to explain my presence. This was
true for all work situations except the bank, where
it was possible to simply drop in and visit, like
any other member of the public who happens to be
acquainted with the people who work there.
The bulk of the data collected came from interviews, repeated interviews with informants and semi-
structured interviews with other workers, who were
paid five dollars for their time. In most cases,
these interviews took place in workers' homes, after
work. Although of course efforts were made to
establish rapport and create an atmosphere of mutual
trust, most of these interviews were rather formal
in tone. This was primarily due to my procedure of
taking copious notes, copying down the gist of
everything they said, often using direct quotes.
Since I do not take shorthand, it was necessary for
the workers to speak slowly or pause often. Generally, they became accustomed to this, and the

11

importance which I seemed to attach to everything
they said was apparently more flattering and rap-
port-enhancing than alienating. It did mean, however, that these interviews, even the almost totally
unstructured first interviews with informants, had a
formal for-the-record quality about them that mocks
the traditional sociological label of this kind of
interview as "informal."

In addition to the observation and interviews,
any other available sources of information about
these work situations were also used. These docu-
mentary sources included annual reports, some memos
addressed from management to their workers, standard
Wall Street references such as Moodys, publications
of local planning agencies and chambers of commerce,
and a teller's training manual.

As sources of comparative data, I decided to
use the notes from interviews that had been conducted during the pre-test phase of the research, and
also the data from case studies that were begun, but
which had to be aborted, either because permission
to do the research was not granted, or because the
informant decided after a few interviews that the
information he was telling me was too sensitive.*

Additionally, some use was made of "existing
data" in the development of the theory, although
little of this is presented in the final research
report. The principal existing data that I had to
work with was my previous work experience as a
printer. There were other short-term jobs, but my
career as a printer was mainly pursued in three
different jobs that each lasted for a period of

---

*These latter cases were omitted from the descriptions of
work situations presented in Chapter 4.

Most dramatically in these two cases, but also in
unreported aspects of the cases I do discuss, many of
these corporate and governmental employers regularly and
routinely broke the law in the course of their daily operations. Some of my informants who reported such activities did not appear to be aware that they were illegal.
Most, however, did recognize the illegality, and thus had
become criminals in the eyes of the law because their
jobs required them to either carry out such illegal activities themselves or to possess guilty knowledge of the
illegal activities carried out for their employer by
others. This phenomenon is worth further exploration, and
I mention it here in hopes that somebody will be hereby
moved to explore it.

about two years. These were an apprenticeship in the composing department of a university press, work as a compositor for a newspaper, and work as an off-set cameraman/stripper for a typographical service. Other sources of existing data were descriptions in the literature of various work situations (Watson, 1971; Valmeras, 1971; Roy, 1955, 1960; Gouldner, 1954; Bensman and Gerver, 1964; Kolaja, 1960; Lasson, 1971), conversations with friends and relatives, and one novel, Harry Swados' On The Line (1958).

Methods and Ethics: Confidentiality and Problems of Access

A standard piece of advice for would-be researchers of work situations is to obtain "dual entry" by getting research permission from management and also from the union, if there is one. The first months of this research were wasted in fruitless effort to follow this advice, and I now tend to agree with Roy (1970) that such a thing is almost always either impossible or inadvisable. Of the dozens of lower level management and union representatives that I approached (after careful preparation had been made through the cultivation of mutual acquaintances to serve as references and contacts), none felt able to agree to such a thing without explicit formal permission from superiors in the organization.*

Even without this experience, I had realized that the traditional dual-entry approach needed to be expanded to a triple-entry system. In other words, I was aware that permission of the union and of management was not sufficient to ensure access to particular work situations. A third access, a relationship of mutual trust with at least one

---

*Friends and relatives who were aware of my problem introduced me to several men who were either top corporate executives or owners of smaller companies. Although some of these men indicated at least an initial willingness to cooperate, I declined their invitations because I was dubious of the validity of any information I might collect from workers under such initial sponsorship in the organization. Although it felt like the right decision to make each time I declined, as I grew increasingly desperate there were periods when I doubted that I had made the right judgement in these cases. I am still uncertain about this.

respected member of the communal network of the particular work place, was necessary. Time and again, the permissions of management and union were not forthcoming, and the work place informant, with whom I had by this time usually conducted a formal interview and at least one informal interview, felt that he could not continue to participate in the study in the face of this explicit refusal of permission.

As the experience and data from these false starts began to accumulate, I became increasingly aware that the working knowledge, and the work decisions that were made as a result of that knowledge, were underground phenomena in these work places, operating often with the tacit acquiescence of the foremen, but not known to anybody in management above that level and illegitimate in terms of the authority structure of the formal organization. Although at this stage of the research my insights were only vague and intuitive, I became increasingly certain that working knowledge added to workers' autonomy and decreased their alienation. I began to feel that to reveal this knowledge to management, to force formal acknowledgement of the existing tacit arrangements, would severely damage these survival mechanisms that the workers had built up. Ironically, the workers, who seemed to have the most to lose from cooperating with this research, were the only ones who were happy to cooperate.

Because I was not getting formal permission from people in authority anyway, and because I began to see the necessity of protecting my informants from the consequences that might ensue if I revealed what they had told me to management, I began to consider the idea of conducting this research "unobtrusively" at least in reference to people in positions of authority. (Webb, et al, 1966) In this situation, perhaps "underground" is a better term than "unobtrusive."

At any rate, when a mutual acquaintance introduced me to my first informant in the Cone Department, I discussed the problem with her and asked if she were willing to participate in the research under these conditions. She was certain that the management at Great Eastern would in fact refuse permission, and she was also certain that she would be fired if her participation in the research was

14

discovered, but she nevertheless agreed to cooperate.*

The decision to conduct the research underground required certain modifications in the original
data collection design. The observations had to be
unobtrusive, and therefore necessarily briefer than
originally planned, and the only sampling procedure
that was possible in selecting workers for interviews was a snowball procedure, whereby workers who
had already built up a relationship of trust with
me in the interview process agreed to introduce me
to a fellow worker. This led to some bias in the
sample, most importantly because all the workers
interviewed had been in their work departments for a
long enough period of time to establish relations of
trust with their co-workers. Another result of my
decision to go underground was the necessity of
abandoning my plan to also interview foremen or
other first-line supervisors. In my opinion, this
was the most regrettable consequence of the decision,
from the point of view of attempting to ensure the
validity of the data collected.

Although I view this decision to go underground
as the only ethical solution to the problem of protecting my worker informants -- my "research subjects" -- there are other aspects of the decision
which I find ethically less than perfect. In some
sense, I have studied the behavior of individual
managers without their knowledge. Conceptually
what I have done is not all that different than a
decision to study them unobtrusively by bugging
their offices.** I must hope that my decision to
disguise the location of this research, a decision
taken basically to protect the informants, will also
be a sufficient protection for them.

---

*Later in the research, I met an anthropologist who had
formerly been an employee of Great Eastern in another
plant and whose request to carry on a much more innocuous
research project than mine, something about the ethnic
backgrounds of the work force, had been turned down.

**Researchers who obtain "permission" from superiors to study
the records or observe the behavior of subordinates are in
exactly the same position, although they have less seldom
recognized the ethnical issue involved.

This decision to conduct the research unobtrusively is important enough to warrant a brief digression. Federal Government research agencies and the American Sociological Association have recently adopted, as a new ethical standard, the position that no research can be conducted without the "informed consent" of the research subjects. This reform was specifically enacted to curb the power of managers and bureaucrats to arbitrarily decide for others how much risk of potential harm is acceptable.*

Yet, if, as in this study, bureaucratic organizations are the research "subjects" as well as bureaucratic employees, then the managers of these organizations, by exercising their right to refuse informed consent, can prevent any research which they deem to have potential policy implications not in their interest. By accepting this new ethical standard, scientists have given over to nonscientist elites the right of veto power over scientific research. If a project of social science inquiry requires the researcher to enter the sphere of influence of a management official, and that official refuses consent, then the research is immediately rendered professionally illegitimate, non-fundable and perhaps even non-publishable, regardless of its scientific importance or validity.

A reform intended to curb the power of organizational elites has ended up giving them even more power. To me, this example is a parable, illustrative of the fate of any reform effort that does not lead to a more basic redistribution of power.

Parable or not, the "informed consent" ethical standard has been a troublesome issue for me. By setting it aside, I appear to have aligned myself with those social scientists who have all along defended what I take to be the positivist philosopher-king position that only we scientists should make these decisions since only we are equipped with the necessary expertise to decide. I reject that argument categorically. Nevertheless, I am quite content with the idea that I am better equipped than the managements of the Great Eastern Container Corporation or the Arnold National Bank to decide

_____

*An example of the kind of abuse that this reform was intended to eliminate is the once wide-spread practice of subjecting prisoners to potentially dangerous medical experiments without disclosing to them the nature of the experiments.

what is in the best interest of their employees.
Taking an ethical stance not grounded in Kant's
categorical imperative is discomforting, even alarm-
ing, but it seems an unavoidable risk.

In the bank case study, people in the work community there made decisions about their participation in this research that were unique in all of
the places which I attempted to study. In this
case, the original informant felt a personal commitment to the branch manager, who she thought was
really a member of the informal work community in
that situation, to tell her about the research. If
the informant wanted to do this, I was willing, but
I felt it would mean the end of this particular case
study, as had happened in the past. In this case,
however, the branch manager decided she was willing
to let me do the research. Other low level managers
had decided the same thing before, but unlike them,
she did not feel it was necessary to request permission of her superiors, or even to inform them
that the research was occurring. Given the ever-
present problem of security at the bank, this decision of hers surprised me, but I am grateful to
her for it, since it eased both my data collection
tasks and my conscience.

Although the data-collection decisions made in
this research clearly represent an ethical compromise,* I believe this compromise is the most ethical
solution available in a situation of conflicting
moral obligations to the different groups that might
be affected by this research.

Attempting to protect the research subjects by
preserving their confidentiality also poses some
thorny problems. For ethnographic research reports,
the value and validity (not to mention credibility)
of the research depends on the faithful and accurate
description of the cases. The more faithful and
accurate the description, the more identifiable the
case is to those familiar with it, and the more pre-
carious the research subjects' confidentiality.

---

*An additional worry in the case of the Cone Department is
the question of industrial espionage. I have tried to protect the technological secrets of the company, but since I
have not talked directly to any management personnel about
exactly what is secret and what is not, all I can do is hope
that my efforts not to reveal these secrets have been successful.

This is an insoluble dilemma, similar to the one
faced by psychiatrists who write up case studies.

In an earlier draft of this study, the descriptions of the research settings were explicit enough
so that local residents could identify the cities,
and local businessmen the companies. Presumably,
had they seen it, company managers could have recognized the departments. Because I wanted to live
up to my assurances of confidentiality (and also
because, why not admit, publishers wanted a shorter,
cheaper book), much descriptive detail has been cut
from this version. Other social scientists might
have decided this issue differently, but the necessity of protecting informants weighs more heavily
on those of us who take a conflict perspective of
the way organizations are run.

I hope this fuller-than-usual discussion of
ethical issues has not been overly labored. My
decision to emphasize it has been deliberate. Just
as the progress of social science has been held back
by by the old convention that research reports
should re-write the research's history to make it
conform to current norms of proper research design,
so have social science ethics been held back by the
convention that there is a single known standard of
research ethics which researchers should simply as a
matter of course imply that they have adhered to.
Doing well and doing right are not that easy in
everyday life, nor are they in scientific research.

The Format of the Work

The findings of the research are presented here
in two parts. Part I contains descriptions of the
work situations studied and the working knowledge
discovered. Included are two case studies, one of a
work department in a paper products factory and the
other a branch bank. These describe the work situations, and the working knowledge of the machine
operators and bank tellers, the principal jobs is
the two work situations. The case study descriptions are based on large amounts of data collected
in each case over a period of several months of
observation, semi-structured interviews with workers, and less structured interviews with a smaller
number of informants.

Chapter 4 presents brief descriptions of ten
other work situations. These are all based on
interviews with one or two informants. Thus, not

only are the presentations briefer than the case
studies, but the data collected about each work
situation are much less complete. The study of each
of these work situations was undertaken either as a
part of the pretesting of the interview schedules
(three work situations) or as an ultimately unsuccessful attempt to gain access to the work situation in order to undertake a full scale case study.
The data collected about these work situations were
therefore originally a side effect of the case study
research, but these "mini" studies eventually provided an invaluable source of comparative data which
I used to check out explanations and generalizations
that emerged from the analysis of the case studies.*
     Part II contains an analysis of working knowl-
edge. This "sociological account" presents a
variety of concepts that increase our understanding
of working knowledge and its effects on the lives of
workers and the operation of work organizations.
This account contains several major elements. Chapter 5 presents a typology of subject areas of working knowledge which may be used in the analytical
description of any individual job holder's stock of
working knowledge. It also presents an explanation
of between-job differences in the amount of working
knowledge necessary, one that accounts for these
differences by referring to characteristics of the
work tasks assigned to jobs in the division of labor
and design of production in the work organization.
Chapter 6 examines the relationship between working
knowledge and work alienation, explaining alienation -- actually, the relative lack of alienation --
by referring to some of the social structural and
social psychological effects of the worker's possession of working knowledge. Chapter 7 examines
the interrelation of knowledge and authority or
control over the work process. The relationship
between knowledge and control is by no means a
simple one: it is true that "knowledge is power,"
but it is also true that control over the division
of labor is also control over access to learning

---

*Actually, twelve work situations in addition to the case
studies were studied in some detail. Two of these work
situations are not presented here, however, because of
promises I made to informants whose increasing concern over
the sensitivity of the information they had given me led
them to request that I not report it, even in pseudonymous
form.

opportunities. Chapter 8 is a summary of the analytical elements, generalizations, and propositions
made in more discursive form in the previous three
chapters. The last chapter discusses some of the
implication of this research for current social
science controversies and social policy issues in
the study of the work process.

Part I
Working Knowledge Described

Introductory Note

The humble purpose of the chapters in Part I
is to provide straight descriptions of the work
situations studied during the course of this research. Although analysis and description are in-
separably linked, a deliberate effort has been made
to avoid extended analysis in Part I. Difficult as
it was to resist the temptation to launch into an
immediate discussion of the important theoretical
issues raised by the material presented in descriptive passages, it seemed worth-while to postpone
these discussions until Part II, where they can be
fitted into a more coherent analytical framework.
The descriptive material presented here has, therefore, been chosen because of its relevance to the
issues raised by the analysis in Part II, but the
analysis itself is not presented here.
    The work descriptions in Part I are intended to
be useful for two purposes. First, they provide the
empirical grounding, the fund of examples and illustrations from a variety of work contexts, for the
theoretical discussion in Part II. Second, the
sociological literature lacks such detailed etho-
graphic accounts of the work situations of the lower
level, blue collar and white collar jobs that employ
the majority of American workers.* Such accounts

---

*Although the early work of Hughes and his students at the
University of Chicago emphasized the study of "low status"
occupations, they deliberately chose occupations in which the
worker was relatively "free" of organizational constraints,
a type of work situation not common then and even less so
today (Hughes, 1958). Most sociologists have confined their
research efforts to those situations (in academic or service-
oriented bureaucracies) to which sociologists have access in
the course of the regular practice of their profession.

are useful, both as tools in the teaching of the sociology of work and as possible comparative grounding for other analysts studying the work process from other perspectives.

The presentation of the cone department and the bank case studies both follow the same format. First the work situation is described, then the working knowledge of the people who hold the principle job within the work situation. These two elements, the work situations and the working knowledge of the people in them, are in a classical dialectical relation. The work situations determine the content of the working knowledge necessary on the job, and the working knowledge becomes a principal means enabling workers to affect their work situations. To say the same thing in a more traditional way, the direct relations of production determine the consciousness of the workers involved, and the workers' activity, guided by this consciousness, helps shape these production relations. (Marx, 1964)

In the chapters describing the two work situations, the key elements selected for description are: the social and organizational contexts of the work situation, the technology, the production design and the resulting work flow, the division of labor, the formal authority structure, and the incentive systems. Because they are so crucial to any study of work behavior or workers' attitudes, all of these elements have been the subjects of intensive previous research in the fields of industrial sociology and formal organizations. This previous literature informs the description of the work situations, as indeed it does all the rest of this study, but the descriptive material as presented here looks forward to the theoretical formulations presented later in the work, not backwards to the previous formulations of others.

After the chapters describing the work situations and the working knowledge in the cone department and the bank, the two principal case studies of this research, the last chapter in Part I presents thumb nail sketches of the other less thoroughly investigated work situations. These descriptions of other blue and white collar work situations provide the reader with additional comparative material that was used in the formation of the generalizations made in Part II. Aside from their intrinsic interest, these descriptions are necessary so that reference can be made to them without breaking up the flow of the argument.

24

2. The Cone Department of the Great Eastern Container Corporation

The Cone Department is a small part of the Great Eastern Container Corporation's old Tanner Street plant in Easton.* The city of Easton is a large and long-established Eastern industrial and commercial center. Its diversified base of heavy industry has for generations now sustained a relatively prosperous economy and a relatively stable blue collar population. Though it is a city of immigrants -- European ethnics, whites from Appalachia, blacks from the South -- it has become a settled place, where people raise their children in the old neighborhoods of flats and rowhouses where they themselves grew up. Church and community organizations are plentiful and securely established. Each ward is a political base for a local family "machine" and the city is governed at the ordinarily accepted levels of competence and corruption. Wages are low, but so are rents, and the city's "disadvantaged" are less likely to be welfare families than members of the working poor.

Most who work in the Cone Department fit in this category, since Great Eastern's pay scale is low even by Easton standards, averaging only a dime or two over the minimum wage. Good pay is not the reason people come to work at Tanner Street. Most come because they already have family that work there, or because it is within walking distance of home, or because the job security is good. Those who stay on, at least in the Cone Department, do so primarily because they like each other's company. Almost everybody says that the best thing about their job is the other people they get to work with.

---

*All names of places, organizations, and individuals have been changed to protect the identity of informants.

Great Eastern has been in existence about fifty years; the Tanner Street Plant was established soon after World War II. Although family controlled by the children of the founder, it is a public corporation, and quite a large one. _Fortune_ magazine lists it among the one thousand largest in the country. Since the fifties, it has been growing vigorously, expanding product lines and spinning off new subsidiaries, until it has by now become a transnational company, with dozens of subsidiaries operating out of plants spread all over the world. By and large, this rapid expansion has been internally generated and conservatively financed. Yet despite all the reinvested capital this has required, dividends distributed to stockholders have been quite high for years. In short, Great Eastern is a well managed, dynamic, and genuinely successful capitalist corporation.

You would be surprised to hear that, though, from a first look at the Tanner Street complex, a sprawling miscellany of Nineteenth-century industrial lofts taking up several blocks in Easton's oldest industrial district. The appearance is deceiving -- Tanner Street is an economically vital, rapidly expanding facility. As other companies in the area shut down their plants, Great Eastern buys them up one by one, installing in each some new department or subsidiary. Inside these old buildings, almost a thousand employees, most of them working with the latest labor-saving machinery, produce everything from heavy machinery to molded plastics to hardware to paper products.

Partly because the plant is so diversified and each department's work so dissimilar, it has been impossible to organize a union at Tanner Street, although there have been recurrent attempts over the years. Until recently unionization was also hindered by the personalistic paternalism of the founder, who knew the older workers by name and attended their weddings and funerals. But the only remnants of this paternalism now are a Christmas bonus and a no-lay-offs policy, both of which continue to appeal to some workers.

If the Cone Department is any indication, most workers at Tanner Street live in the inner-city neighborhoods located all around this manufacturing area, black neighborhoods to the west and white ones to the east. Many live farther away in the city or suburbs, though, and a few commute as far as one hundred miles each way from depressed rural areas to the south. The workforce is about sixty percent

white and about forty percent black, but in the
worst jobs these proportions are reversed. This one
ethnic distinction is clearly maintained, but other
ethnic divisions are no longer significant. The
ethnic backgrounds of white workers are known to
others as part of their identity, but these cultural
symbols do not have the divisive force they once had.
The only casually expressed ethnic prejudice in the
plant is anti-Semitism, perhaps because the top
management is predominantly Jewish, and there are no
longer any other Jewish workers to worry about
offending.

The Cone Department: An Introduction

The Cone Department gets its name from its one
product -- paper cones. Mainly, these are used as
containers for single servings of food or beverage:
cotton candy, snow cones, frozen ice cream cones,
french fries, soda fountain drinks, water, cream for
coffee. Using slightly different machines, the
department makes two different kinds of cones,
"heavies" (like soda fountain cups) and "lights"
(like cotton candy holders), named after the weight
of paper used. The main work floor of the department is therefore divided into two banks of machines,
the "heavy side" and the "light side," each with its
own corps of workers. In a separate "taps" room, a
few women operate other machines that make tops and
caps ("taps") for some of the cones.
Essentially, the work of the Cone Department is
to take two-ton rolls of paper, coat it, print it,
cut and fold and glue it into cones, and to pack
them for shipment to the customer. This batch processing of a raw material to produce a more valuable
finished product is the archetype of industrial
manufacture. It therefore has many features in common with this type of production in other industries
(Woodward, 1965). The one unusual aspect of the
Cone Department is the scope of the production process that it includes, all the way from raw material
to finished product. It is more common in industry
for the work flow to be organized so that different
departments work on successive stages of production
(cf. Blauner, 1964, 23).

The Division of Labor

The tasks of the Cone Department have been
divided among workers according to two classical
principals of capitalist rationality. First, the

27

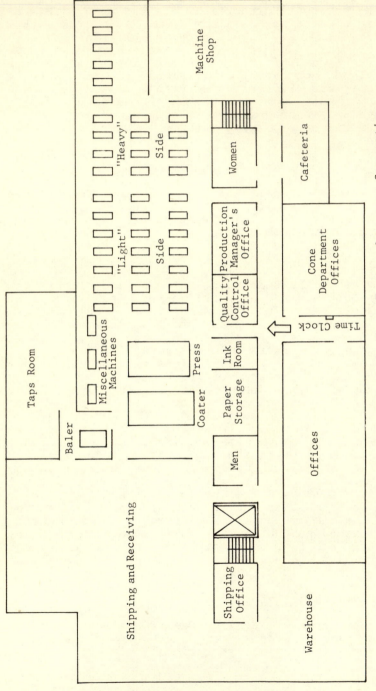

Floor Plan, Cone Department of the Great Eastern Container Corporation

APPROXIMATE NUMBER OF CONE DEPARTMENT WORKERS,
BY SHIFT, JOB CATEGORY, AND SEX

Job Category:	First Shift	Second Shift	Third Shift	Total
Machine operators				
Light side	19	18	12	49 (all women)
Heavy side	13	12	7	32 (all women)
Relief	2	2	1	5 (all women)
Taps room	2	2	4	18 (all women)
Material handlers	6	5	4	15 (3 women; 12 men)
Inspectors	2	2	1	5 (all women
Inkmen	2	2	1	5 (all men)
Mechanics on floor (includes shift leader)	6	5	3	14 (1 woman trainee; 13 men)
Machinists in shop	10	--	--	10 (all men)
Coater machine operators	2	2	2	6 (all men)
Totals	64	5u	35	149

(These are the average number of people actually working during
a particular shift, given normal rates of absenteeism and
temporary vacancies due to turn-over.)

machines must be kept running at all times. Therefore, the work must be organized so that machine
operators need never leave their machines. Second,
labor costs must be minimized. Therefore, the work
tasks that still require highly skilled workers must
be collected together into as few jobs as possible,
or to put it another way, the most skilled work tasks
must be removed from as many jobs as possible. This
permits the cheapest possible ratio of highly paid
"skilled" workers to poorly paid "unskilled" workers.
So faithfully have these two principals been followed in this case that the Cone Department may be regarded in this respect as archetypical of machine-
tending work as it was organized in the days before
cybernetic technology and "human relations" managerial ideology.
    The particular application of these principals
in the Cone Department has resulted in a division of
labor based on five major job categories. The two

29

low-paying jobs are machine operators and material handlers. Machine operators tend the machines, check for defects, and pack the products as they come off the machines. Material handlers supply the machines with raw materials, remove the cases of finished cones, and take care of any miscellaneous chores that come up. The three more highly paying jobs are mechanics, inkmen, and quality control inspectors. Mechanics are in charge of maintaining and repairing the machines. A senior mechanic on each shift serves as shift leader. Inkmen* set up and maintain the printing units built into each machine, changing over the printing plate and ink colors when a machine finishes one customer's order and must be made ready to begin another. Quality control inspectors circulate through the shop, sampling each operator's production to check for defects.

Machine operators have been assigned three production functions: inspecting the cones or wrappers for defects; packing them in boxes (250 to a box) and cases (20 boxes to a case); and tending the machine, keeping its critical working surfaces clean. If the machine jams, breaks-down, or begins to produce defective cups, they are supposed to shut down the machine to see if a routine cleaning will solve the problem. If it won't, they are supposed to shut it down again and call a mechanic or (for printing defects) an inkman. They are definitely not supposed to attempt to repair the machine themselves, nor are they expected to know how to do this. Although not formally responsible for quantity of production, since they are not the ones who keep the machines in running condition, they are responsible for the quality of the cones they pack. On each case they put a label which identifies the machine and the operator.

Material Handlers, informally called "paper boys" by the operators, are responsible for servicing the machines, threading new rolls of paper into the machine when the old rolls run out and keeping the glue pots full. They also hand-truck the finished cases out into the shipping department, where they sort them according to customer orders and stack them on separate skids. They are also responsible for keeping the area around the machines on their side clean, and for separating trash and debris into

---

*The sex-identifying job title reflects both actual shop floor usage and the real sexual division of labor.

recycleable paper, which is thrown into the paper-baler's vacuum system, and regular trash, which is deposited in dumpsters. They oversee the operation of the baler and its vacuum, clearing out jams when they occur. In general, they are responsible for all the odd jobs around the shop that aren't definitely somebody else's job, in addition to their primary function of servicing the machines.

The division of labor between machine operators and material handlers originally served to permit the employment of lower paid women machine operators, since all the "heavy work" was done by male material handlers. The present wage scale still reflects the original sexual division of labor, since the rate for operators ranges from $2.32-$2.70 per hour, while the material handlers' rate is from $2.70-$2.77. The belief that the material handler's job is heavy work derives from the weight of the paper rolls (up to 250 pounds). Material handlers don't actually lift the roll, though, without the aid of a paper jack, a simple piece of apparatus that works on the lever principle. Glinnis, the female material handler who was interviewed, says that it doesn't require brute strength to use the paper jack.

> There's a trick. You've got to jerk the handle quick and it (the paper roll) will pop right up there.... If they tried to do it gradually even strong guys couldn't do it.

As Glinnis and two other women have recently found out, there is nothing in the material handler's job that can not be physically handled by a normal woman.

All the quality control inspectors are former machine operators. When a production run begins, they check and see that the initial production meets the customer's specifications, especially with regard to size of the product and the placement, color, and opacity of its printed label. Their other responsibility is to spot check each machine's production two or three times a day. They look for three main types of defects: defects in the construction of the cones, defects in the printing, and material defects in the paper used.

Built into most machines is a color offset printing press, which the inkmen call a "unit printer." Inkmen are basically responsible for setting up these mini-presses for each job, installing the right printing plates, mixing and loading the right colors of ink, and setting the register so that

each color is printed in the right place in relation
to the product and to the other colors. First-
shift inkmen receive instructions about what new
jobs should be set up each day directly by telephone
from the central office. A sub-contracting plate-
maker makes the printing plates and delivers them
to the inkmen. In addition to setting up the new
job runs, inkmen and their helpers are responsible
for re-setting the machines periodically during the
run when they go more than 1/16th inch out of register, for cleaning the plates periodically as the dust
and dried ink accumulates, for re-filling the ink
wells, and for generally maintaining and repairing
the unit printers.

Mechanics perform many distinct work tasks, only
some of which involve the simple repair of machines.
Mechanics at different grade levels do different
jobs. At the lowest level, machine adjusters are on
call when the operators first detect trouble. Many
of the problems are relatively routine things, like
changing blades, which the machine adjustor can take
care of. Other times, however, he either cannot
identify the source of the problem or he does not
know how to fix it. In these cases he calls over
the production mechanic working with him on that
particular side. The production mechanic is called
that because he is lowest level worker in the shop
that has actual "production responsibility," that is,
who is held accountable for his side's rate of production. Nevertheless, his basic job is still only
to repair malfunctioning machines. Some production
mechanics are called senior production mechanics
because they have worked there longer, know more,
and are paid more.

Three of the senior production mechanics are
shift leaders for the three shifts. Each is responsible for production rates on his shift in general
and for meeting the particular deadlines that some
of the rush order jobs carry. He assigns operators
to the various machines at the beginning of the
shift, and picks the operators who will serve as
relief operators.* He also is responsible for over-

_____

*Although each operator normally runs "her" machine, there
are inevitable complications at the beginning of each
shift, because certain jobs on certain machines have
higher priority than other jobs, and because three or four
of the operators are normally absent on any given
shift.

32

seeing the activities of the material handlers and
mechanics on his shift. Since he is the most
experienced mechanic on hand, especially on the
second and third shifts when the machine shop is
closed, he also undertakes the most difficult repairs. The shift leader has a hectic, tense job.
Some of the senior mechanics have refused to take
it, and some have tried it for a while and then quit
to go back to being a regular mechanic.
    The most technically skilled mechanics are
called machinists, and work most of their time in the
machine shop. Many of the basic parts to the machines are built right in the machine shop. This is the
shop's main activity, but major repairs that require
a large portion of a machine to be torn down and re-
built are performed by machinists at their benches.
The machine shop only works the first shift, and it
has its own working foreman and its own supervisor.

Production Design

    The social organization of work in the Cone
Department results as much from the design of the
work flow and the choice of machinery as it does
from the division of labor. The most important production design decision was the invention of a unique
machine that performs almost every step in the cone
making process. The concept is similar to the design
of a modern large press specialized in the printing
of high-volume paperback books. Printing, cutting,
folding, and binding operations, which in less
specialized shops would be handled by separate
machines, are combined into one big machine that
takes in rolls of blank paper at one end and puts
out finished books at the other. Likewise, cone
machines combine a number of distinct operations to
accomplish their highly specialized purpose, the
making of cones. They print, cut, glue, shape, and
finish the cones in one continuous operation.
    How do these machines work? How are the cones
actually made? Paper arrives from the mill in huge
rolls. These rolls are run through a coater machine,
which moistens the paper, applies a wax coating, and
slits the mill rolls into narrow cone rolls. Material handlers load these rolls onto individual cone
machines and thread the paper through the machines.
    Once loaded, the operator starts her machine,
and the long narrow strip of paper unwinds off its
roll, endlessly into the machine, where the first
element it encounters is an offset printing press.
In this operation, a photographically prepared

INDIVIDUAL FUNCTIONS IN THE WORK FLOW OF PRODUCTION
IN THE CONE DEPARTMENT

Function	Machine used	Workers responsible	Auxiliary functions & workers
1. Receiving paper, ink, & raw materials.		Shipping department	
2. Coating the paper.	Coater	Coater operators	Loading, unloading & maintain-coater: coater operators
3. Moistening the paper.			
4. Slitting the mill rolls into individual rolls.			
5. Wrapping rolls in plastic to prevent drying out.		Coater operators	
6. Transporting rolls to machines & threading them up.		Material handlers	
7. Printing	Cone machines	Machine operators	Supplying & setting up inks & plates: inkmen. Filling glue pots: material handlers. Cleaning machine: operators. Maintaining machine: mechanics
8. Cutting the cone			
9. Applying glue.			
10. Shaping.			
11. Edging.			
12. Inspection for defects.		Machine operators	Checked by inspectors
13. Packing cones into boxes & cases.		Machine operators	
14. Labeling cases.		Machine operators	
15. Taping & sealing cases		Material handlers	
16. Removing cases to appropriate pallets in shipping room.		Material handlers	
17. Loading trucks & shipping out.		Shipping Department	

printing plate, wrapped around a cylinder, first contacts a water roller, which wets the plate except
where the chemicals on the plate repel the water.
Next the printing cylinder passes by an ink roller,
which leaves ink only in those dry areas which have
not been wet by the water roller. The inked plate
then comes in contact with a special rubber "offset"
cylinder which receives the ink pattern and transfers
it to the paper as it passes over this offset cylinder. The paper then passes on to a second color
printer which repeats this operation completely (for
a job that calls for printing in two colors, as most
of them do). The positioning of the impression
plates on their cylinders, and the timing of the
cylinder rotations in relation to each other determine the relative position of the different colors.
This relative position is called "register," and is
a delicately maintained thing. As the machine goes
through thousands of revolutions, any minute error
in timing or position can grow rapidly into a readily
visible defect. The inkmen claim that the timing
mechanisms of these old machines are sufficiently
sloppy to go a little out of register every time the
machine is started or stopped.

Next, the printed web passes over a moving
platen while a knife, moving in a mechanically pre-
determined path, cuts out the product shape from the
rest of the web. The left-over paper, still continuous along its edges, passes into the vacuum
system to be sucked directly from the machine to the
department's waste paper baler. The piece of paper
which will form the cone is gripped by small suction
devices in the platen, called "titties" by the workers because of their shape, and passed under the glue
nozzles that spray the glue pattern onto those parts
of the paper which will have to be stuck together
after it is folded. Then, the paper is passed over
a rotating cone-shaped mold, called the "head" of
the machine. The paper is pushed into the mold by a
piece of metal called a "pecker," suction devices
draw the paper into tight conformity with the shape
of the mold, the glue sets, and the product has
acquired its basic shape. By this time the head has
nearly completed its rotation and has reached the
proper position to expel the cone into a chute.
The cone nestles into the previous cone and propels
the row of cones in the chute along a fraction of an
inch further. This chute leads along the side of
the machine to the edger, a final operation fitted
on most of the machines, where the exposed paper

edges are curled so that they will not cut people
the way that unfinished paper edges occasionally do.

Thus, the machine incorporates three clearly
distinct functions, the central cutting/glueing/shap-
ing function, the initial printing and the final edging. In fact, only the central function is performed
on all products; some orders call for plain unprinted
paper, and others require only the cheaper, flimsier,
unedged products. In addition to this division of
functions, moreover, it is obvious that the cutting,
glueing, and shaping are grouped together only by
their close physical and temporal proximity. They
are distinct processes each with their own distinct
technologies.

As the products come out of the edger and pile
up in the machine's final chute, there still remain
two essential tasks to be performed in the production
process. The operator must inspect the cones for defects and pack them into boxes. These last two tasks
are still carried on by the operators themselves,
unaided by any machinery. These two functions are
the subjects of most of the formal or legitimate
knowledge that operators are expected by management
to acquire. Most of the considerable knowledge about
the machine and its parts that operators acquire is
formally considered to be part of the mechanics'
work role.

The inspection requires a special 'knack.' The
operator picks up a stack of cones and "bridges" them
in such a way that, as the cones are arched over
from one hand to the other, each is separated from
the stack for a split second and rotated by a quick
movement of the thumb. This bridging operation, combined with the operator's knowledge of what possible
defects to look for and the acute visual sensitivity
to minute differences in the cones which each operator develops, makes it possible to visually inspect
a stack of a hundred cups in two or three seconds.
Operators can spot deviations from the expected
pattern created as each twirling cup emerges for an
instant from within its predecessor. This operation
is quite spectacular to watch, and would do credit
to any accomplished magician or card shark, but to
the operators it is just part of the job. "Light"
cones are not stiff enough to be bridged, and they
must be "tumbled," a similar operation which involves
holding a stack in the upper hand while spinning and
dropping the wrappers one by one into the lower hand.
The effect is the same as in bridging, but the wrappers are dropped vertically instead of being arched
horizontally from hand to hand.

To pack the cones, the operator must weigh a
stack of cups on a scale pre-set with each new paper
roll, adding or removing cones until it contains the
weight equivalent of 250 cones, slipping the stack
into a cardboard box, and inserting the box in an
open case. When a case is full, the operator labels
it to identify the product, the customer, and the
order number, then she writes in her own code number
and the machine code. While the machine is running,
a majority of the operator's time is spent going
through the physical motions of packing the cones,
but there is less skill and working knowledge called
for by this function than by either the machine-tending or the quality control functions.

The Production Control System

The only difference between customers' orders
or "jobs" is that different printing plates and
different printing inks are used. The change over
from one job to the next is a simple matter, involving only a routine cleaning and plate change on the
part of the inkman. The department is set up to
produce different sizes of products, but every effort
is made in the scheduling of production to avoid
having to change one machine over from one size to
another, since this is a lengthy and costly process
that takes a skilled machinist the better part of a
shift to accomplish.
The steps that the department goes through to
get a new job into production are as follows. The
order is sent over from the headquarters plant in
Waltham, and the plates are delivered by the plate-
maker. The inkmen and the shift leader, and sometimes the production manager, confer with each other,
assessing the progress being made on the current jobs
in the shop and deciding which of the appropriately
set-up machines will be free soon enough to take on
the new one. The company has several long-standing
customers who regularly reorder the same product with
the same specifications. The department runs these
jobs more or less constantly, trying to stockpile in
slack times. These standing jobs and their stock-
piles give the men who make the production scheduling
decisions the kind of flexibility they need in their
efforts to reconcile three conflicting goals: minimizing change-overs, keeping the machines running,
and still meeting deadlines on rush and priority
jobs. Once the machine has been chosen and the old
job on that machine has finished its run, the inkman
makes the change-over. The shift leader provides

the operator with the new labels that she needs to mark the finished cases. The old "production card" is taken off its hook next to the machine and sent into the production manager's office, and the inkman hangs on a new production card for the new job. The machine is started up again, and the inspectors take some of its initial production back into their office to check the colors and plate registration against the job specifications. After their okay, the new job is in production. If the inkman can work without being interrupted by repair calls, the change-over normally takes about an hour and a half.

The production cards are shift-by-shift accounts of the production progress on the job and of the events in the lives of the operators and their machine which effected the production. These running records form the only objective basis for management's knowledge about the department's production processes and its day-to-day functioning. They are important symbols in the department's work culture, key objects of working knowledge for the operators and (to a lesser extent) mechanics.

At the end of every shift, the operators fill in their production cards, noting the number of cases produced on that shift and writing up machine malfunctions that resulted in the accumulation of machine "down time" during the course of the shift. The number of cases produced is added cumulatively and allows anyone to see at a glance how many cases are left to go in the run. Once the run is complete, the production cards are filed in the production manager's office. There, they are the basis on which it is possible for management to compare production records of operators. Although this is not ordinarily done, the operator interviews demonstrate their strong awareness of this possibility. As one put it:

> I keep pushing them (the mechanics)
> until they get it right, and then I write
> everything down on the cards so they can
> see how long it took before I got my
> machine back running right again.

In general, the operators try to document down time. This is encouraged by the mechanics, who occasionally help a semi-literate operator with her write-up, because the production cards also serve as a record of the repairs on each machine. Faced with a cantankerous machine, mechanics look back through the record to see what mechanics on other shifts

38

have tried. Occasionally, the shift leader or a machinist will go look through the old production cards to see how long it has been since a machine has been overhauled or particular parts replaced.

The Formal Authority Structure

The management hierarchy of the cone department is a three-tiered structure, with separate lines of authority for the department as a whole and the machine shop. In the machine shop, there is both a working foreman and a shop superviser, Morty, the man whom the workers believe invented the cone machines and the person in the department most respected by the workers. The quality control inspectors likewise have their own working "forelady," the most senior person in her job. All the rest of the department's workers are supervised by the senior mechanic shift-leaders on each shift. The shift leaders and the chief inspector report to the Production Manager, Roger Blum, who shares an office with his secretary out in the hall, away from the noise and paper dust of the shop floor. In a larger and fancier suite of offices even further away is Anthony Prezzi, the Department Manager and direct superior for Roger Blum and Morty.*

Because the research situation did not permit interviews with anybody in management, it is not possible to describe the formal areas of responsibility for each position. Workers had only very vague ideas of the various responsibilities of these men, and were generally convinced that Anthony Prezzi and Roger Blum didn't do much of anything:

> (Anthony) doesn't do nothing. Take it from me, he doesn't know nothing. That man doesn't know nothing from nothing about this department.... A good thing he doesn't do nothing because everytime he does come in and do something, it just fucks somebody up.

> I don't know what (Roger) does do in his office. Now that you mention it, I wonder what he is supposed to be doing when he's not

---

*Though changed here to protect indentities, these names follow the format of workers' usage. Workers refer to the machine shop superviser by his first name, Morty, while the other two managers are known as "Blum" and "Prezzi."

out with us. Not that he does anything
when he's out of his office either.

This attitude is partly a reflection of a normal
attitude of production workers towards desk workers,
partly a reflection of the accurate realization that
the "management" co-ordination functions immediately
necessary to production are handled by the shift
leaders and the workers themselves. Other factors
that obscure the managers' roles are their laissez
faire management style, lack of consistent exercise
of control, and the fact that the actual (as opposed
to the formal) lines of authority are tangled and
ambiguous.
     Examples of ambiguous lines of authority can be
found at all levels in the shop. For instance, in
technical matters, Morty has more authority over
mechanics than either their formal boss, the shift
leader, or his boss, the production manager. (See
Crozier, 1964, 107 ff, for a similar example of
mechanical experts receiving more actual authority
than the nominal managers.) The only practical
authority over senior inkmen is the production
manager, not the shift leader. Production mechanics,
who have no formal line authority, only "production
responsibility," frequently act as a fourth layer of
authority interposed over operators and material
handlers.
     It is worth stating in passing one aspect of
authority in the department about which there is no
ambiguity. All these men are men. All operators
are women; all managers are men. (Cf. Acker and Van
Houten, 1974)
     Most of these ambiguities, if not all, can be
traced to ambiguities in the role of mechanic. All
of these men are or were mechanics, except Prezzi,
who rose into management from the shipping department. Mechanics are the only workers responsible
for production. There is a confusion between being
a mechanic and having management responsibilities, a
confusion that is increased by the shift leaders'
use of their senior mechanic colleagues as stand-ins
for management tasks -- for instance, the assignment
of operators to machines at the start of the shift.
     The production manager meets members of all
shifts, because he arrives for work at the end of
the third shift and stays until after the start of
the second shift. This enables him to confer directly with all three shift leaders about production
priorities and difficulties with particular jobs.
The department manager also occasionally comes in

early and leaves late, but not on a regular basis.
Members of the first shift report that Blum is on
the work floor about forty per cent of the time and
Prezzi about ten per cent of the time. When out
there, they regularly give direct orders to operators or, more frequently, material handlers, but
these orders are perceived as concerning relatively
unimportant tasks. Also, these orders frequently
violate informal norms and expectations about work
procedures. This contributes to workers' perceptions of them as arbitrary, and of Prezzi as someone
who "likes to show off his power over you."

Work Shifts and Work Breaks -- The Organization of Time in the Cone Department

On high priority orders, the machines in the
cone department are kept running non-stop all week,
and the work time of the people who service and
operate the machines has been scheduled to facilitate
this continuous operation. The operators work eight-
hour shifts: 8:00 A.M. to 4:00 P.M., 4:00 P.M. to
midnight, midnight to 8:00 A.M. The schedules of
the material handlers, mechanics and inkmen are set
up to overlap, guaranteeing that these people will
have a half-hour or more overtime each day. Each
shift is broken up by three break periods, a half-
hour for lunch and two ten-minute breaks. These
are the only three legitimately permitted breaks,
and the workers are supposed to arrange their personal affairs and their bodily functions so as not
to interfere with the work process on company time.
This company policy is universally ignored however:
"You use the bathroom to get an extra break....
you don't waste your break time that way."
     The start of a new shift and the finish of an
old one follows a habitualized pattern of transition. Thirty to sixty minutes before the new shift
starts, the mechanics, inkmen, and material handlers
start arriving. They punch in, then generally they
move to the cafeteria for a cup of coffee before
going out onto the floor. On the floor, mechanics
and inkmen discuss the current status of the machines
and the job orders on their 'side' with their
counterparts on the previous shift. Twenty minutes
or more before the hour, the first of the operators
arrive. They collect in the cafeteria, waiting until
at least quarter of the hour before punching in, as
company policy requires. They won't start getting
paid in any case until their shift officially begins.

41

Ten minutes or so before the start of the shift, their shift leader or one of the other senior production mechanics comes out into the cafeteria and makes the day's work assignments, deciding who should run which machine and who should work relief. The material handlers, meanwhile, have finished their coffee and have gone out onto the floor, where they spend the last fifteen minutes or so straightening up their side, re-filling each operator's can of cleaning water with fresh water, and generally trying to get their side set up so that they can service it smoothly when they go on. The old shift's material handlers continue to handle any paper changes that might come up during this period. Starting the last two minutes or so before the hour, the operators trickle out onto the floor, look over their machine, exchange a few words about its present condition and temperament with the operator they are relieving, and stand by ready to take over. On the hour, a buzzer sounds, the new operators take over, and the old ones leave. The mechanics and inkmen from the old shift finish up whatever they were doing and gradually move out into the cafeteria, where they sit and wait for their punch-out time at half-past the hour. The transition is complete, and the new shift has begun.

The Training System for New Employees

The training system for machine operators and material handlers normally lasts three days. It consists of a brief lecture in the personnel department about the company and its employment policies, followed by assignment to an experienced worker who will serve as trainer. At the start of the three-day period, trainees watch the experienced worker while he or she goes about the job. By the end of the three-day period the trainer should be watching while the trainee does the job. The quality of the training the new worker gets depends completely on the worker who happened to be assigned this task. There is a great deal of variation in the attitude that the older workers take towards the training assignment. They are not compensated for this extra task, and some of them exact their compensation by making the trainee do the job from the beginning, basically without any supervision. Other workers, on the other hand, take this training assignment very seriously -- seeing it as a chance to have some influence on the future behaviour and work standards of someone with whom they will be working. In the interviews, none of the workers saw any pattern in the shift leaders' choices of people to train the new workers. On each shift there are a definite number of older employees whom the other workers respect as a "good operator," or a "good material handler." Management normally picks these people to train new workers, but frequently enough the training assignment goes to an older worker whose work is not respected in the department.

At the end of the three-day period, the new worker has learned the basic procedures. According to the workers who were interviewed, it takes an additional period ranging from a few weeks to two or three months before workers feel confident in their ability to stay on top of the work. Two elements are involved in this post-training break-in period. The workers must train their fingers to handle the job procedures, which originally are learned in only a theoretical way. The body motions necessary to the packing process must become almost automatic before the new worker can be in comfortable coordination with the speed of her machine. Meanwhile, the break-in period also includes a great deal of "theoretical learning." In this process, the worker learns how the machine operates, so that the defects she was taught to look for in the training period now become understandable and, sometimes, predictable, due to her increasing knowledge of how the machine works and what kind of defects might be caused by what kind of problems. In other words, during the break-in period the procedures and facts about the equipment that she was taught in the training period become rooted in a deeper understanding of her machine and her work role. She acquires the paradigm that makes previously inexplicable novelties seem a natural part of the work environment.

A significant thing about this training program for machine operators and material handlers is the company's willingness to virtually allow old workers to define the job parameters for new workers. A normal characteristic of all work organizations is the existence of a tension between the organization's formal job descriptions of its work roles and the actual working behavior of the people who occupy these work roles. (Crozier, 1964; Gouldner, 1954; Blau, 1955) This tension also exists in the cone department -- operators and material handlers report that there are some things that they "are supposed to do" but don't do -- but is minimized since the company makes remarkably little effort to enforce these work role expectations. For instance, managers never systematically inform new workers of what these expectations are. Typically, the workers only find out about them when the department manager or the production manager unexpectedly invokes some long forgotten norm. For instance, one day the Department Manager noticed some material handlers who were standing around momentarily unoccupied and told them to get busy cleaning up the machines not in use during that particular shift. As a result, a material handler on duty that shift reported that basic machine cleaning is part of the material handlers job, "But we never do it unless somebody makes us." Material handlers not present during that shift, on the other hand, deny that this task is their responsibility at all. Since there are no formal, authoritative norms for each job -- as there might be in a manual or handbook if the department had one -- each worker has a slightly different version of formal job requirements. This idiosyncratic personal understanding is all the worker can pass on to the new worker being trained, and this satisfies the company. To the outside observer, the company's permitting of the workers to run their own training program appears to be an open admission that management does not know in clear detail what the workers in each type of job actually do.

The mechanics' and ink-men's jobs are more complex, the body of working knowledge they must acquire more extensive, and the training program is therefore longer. Each new mechanic or inkman has a three month probationary period, during which time they work more or less under the senior mechanic or inkman on their side. After the first couple of weeks, their job is not much different from any other machine adjuster or inkman's helper except they are not expected to know much, and are expected to call in a senior person more often and for a wider range of problems. The company used to hire only mechanics and inkmen that already "had experience." They were expected to know the job already, but usually did not, since the cone department's operation is fairly specialized. Although no formal policy change has been announced, the mechanics and inkmen hired-on in the last year have been recruited from the male material handlers in the department and already have observed a great deal about their new job before they actually move into it. (One recently hired mechanic is a woman who was formally a machine

44

operator, but the company has resisted allowing other women to make this move, although some machine operators have applied.)

Machine Operators' Working Knowledge

In the cone department, the most routinized work tasks and the lowest wages go to the machine operators. To follow through on the research strategy that led to the cone department in the first place, it is the working knowledge of the machine operators that should be selected as a kind of worst-case test of the general proposition that the working knowledge of "unskilled" workers is a crucial factor of production.*

The machine operator's body of working knowledge forms an integral whole, but for analytic purposes, two types of working knowledge may be distinguished, basic and supplementary. Basic knowledge includes all the procedures necessary to routinely carry out their work tasks: how to start and stop the machine, clean it in the prescribed manner, "bridge" the cones, unfold the boxes, pack the cones, label the cases, etc. Supplementary knowledge includes all the know-how necessary to handle the obstacles to this routine work performance that arise from time to time: how to keep the machine running, overcome "bad" paper, diagnose the cause of defects, keep the inspectors happy, secure the cooperation of mechanics and material handlers, etc. The use of basic knowledge becomes a matter of habitualized routine. Supplementary working knowledge is developed about any physical or social phenomena in the cone department that tend to create problems for machine operators. Supplementary knowledge is consciously applied to resolve these problems so that they do not remain obstacles to routinely efficient production. The fact that every worker must possess

---

*Actually, since they are "operatives," the machine operators are "semi-skilled," according to the Labor Department's technical definition, while the material handlers are "unskilled" laborers. Although data on the working knowledge of both groups were collected, the machine operators are selected here as a worst-case test because Bright's (1971) and Braverman's (1974, 424-449) arguments that higher degrees of mechanization decrease skill levels were more persuasive than the Labor Department's categories.

45

a certain minimum of basic knowledge necessary to do
even highly routinized work will surprise no one.
What managers, social scientists, and even many workers themselves do not realize is the extent of
supplementary knowledge that is also necessary.

For machine operators, the most significant
sources of difficulty and therefore the subject areas
of the most highly developed working knowledge are:
properties of the raw materials that make up the
cones; machine deficiencies, both those designed into all of them and those idiosyncratic to each; the
quality standards of different groups in the department; and the social relations among workers in the
department's various jobs. Only a small sampling of
the working knowledge necessary in each of these
subject areas can be presented, but it ought to be
possible to at least give an insight into the machine
operator's field of study.

Knowledge about materials. The raw materials
for cone-making are paper, ink, and glue. Glue consistency and ink opacity are problematic properties
of these materials. Glue that is too thick, too
thin, or too "lumpy" will either cause defects or
stick the paper to the machine parts, resulting in a
"jam-up." Ink too thin produces washed out colors
that the inspectors might reject, while ink too
thick makes the paper sticky, also a cause of jam-
ups.

Operators hate jam-ups. Defects are to be
avoided, but jam-ups are the bane of the operator's
existence. Every time the machine jams, the operator must shut it off completely, clean out the jam-
med-up paper which has diabolically pushed itself
into all sorts of inaccessible crevices, clean the
machine, rethread the paper off the roll through the
machine to the cutters, and start it up again. If
this process takes too long, then the ink and glue
in the machine have begun to dry out by the time the
machine is restarted, and new problems are compound-
ed on the old problem that originally caused the
jam.

The glue and the ink can cause trouble, but
the raw material that is the most consistent source
of operators' headaches is the paper. The paper
for the cone machines has been pre-moistened and
waxed by the men who operate the coater machine down
at the other end of the department. If, as frequently happens, the paper comes out of this previous

operation too wet, or too dry, or too waxy, then it
creates havoc for the operator and her machine.*

Paper that is too wet makes a poor base for a
quality print job, since it slows down the ink's
drying time and therefore increases the likelihood
of smudging and smearing. The most experienced
operators have learned how to adjust the pressure
of the various rollers in the printing unit to
alleviate this problem. Similarly, wet paper slows
the drying time of the glue, increasing the likelihood of jam-ups in the machine head. Running wet
paper dampens critical parts in the machine, and
this makes it much more difficult to keep the
machine clean and running smoothly. Ink, glue, and
the sludge formed from the mixture of paper dust
and moisture build up more rapidly on damp surfaces.
The knowledgeable operator compensates for wet
paper by: slowing down the machine to give ink and
glue more time to dry, setting up a portable elec-
tric heater to heat the roll of paper as it unwinds
into the machine, making minor machine adjustments,
and keeping the machine especially clean. Running
wet paper also puts a premium on the unsanctioned
and "unsafe" cleaning techniques that these workers
have developed to clean the printing unit rollers
while the machine is still running.

Paper that is too dry loses much of its flexibility. As it winds its way through the machine,
getting cut and bent and molded, the wax coating
cracks. Cups with this kind of cracked wax surface
must be thrown away. The problem is particularly
acute in the edging operation; when the paper is
too dry the cone or wrapper will emerge from the
edger with a rim that is chewed up and ragged instead of smooth. Some operators keep a cup of
clean water from the drinking fountain when they are
running dry paper. They dip a paper towel into the
water and run it across the line of cups and use it
to wet the edges before they go into the final edging process. One operator said in her interview
that she does this even with normal paper, since it
produces a "beautiful smooth" edge that is better
than the machine can turn out otherwise, under even
optimal conditions. Despite the possible defects
that it can produce, however, dry paper is not as

---

*It is worth noting that the whole range of wetness and
waxiness discussed by the operators involves differences
not detectable to the untrained eyes and hands of the outside
observor.

much of a threat to the operators as paper that is too wet or waxy. Dry paper produces only defects; wet or waxy paper produces defects and increases the number of jams and malfunctions that the operator will probably have to deal with.

Paper that is too waxy is too sticky and too thick. Both characteristics can increase the likelihood that the paper will jam the machine. The operators try to compensate for too waxy paper by slowing the machine way down and by adjusting certain rollers so that the extra thickness of the paper can pass through more easily. These adjustments can lessen the likelihood of jam-ups, but they cannot eliminate them altogether. Therefore, the operators' principal strategy to deal with waxy paper is to try to get the material handlers on their side to agree that this particular roll of paper is so waxy that it physically cannot be run at all. If she is successful in this redefinition, the material handler will use his knife to "cut down" the roll, removing the outer inches of paper in hopes that the inner parts of the roll will be less waxy. If the inner layers are not any better, the material handler may keep cutting right down to the core. The paper thus removed is discarded into the vacuum system. Since it is only very rarely the case that the paper is literally so waxy that it cannot be run on the machine, management defines this "cutting down" operation as unnecessary paper waste. On the first shift, therefore, this operation must be done hurriedly, so it can be completed before Anthony Prezzi or Roger Blum happen to stroll by.

Cutting down paper is probably the most physically taxing operation that material handlers are called upon to do. Consequently, the operator has to be quite persuasive to get them to agree to do it at all. Their preferred solution is to have the operator run the machine with the paper not threaded through, that is, with the paper unwinding from the roll directly into the vacuum system. This accomplishes the same thing but takes considerably more time. A second disadvantage for the operator is that all the ink and glue that would normally be applied to the paper is spread all over the insides of the machine, requiring a massive clean-up operation before the machine can be run smoothly again.

Each individual machine roll is only a fraction of a former mill roll that had been run through the coater machine all at once. If one machine roll is too waxy, the whole batch is too waxy. If one

48

operator is having trouble with waxy paper, all of
her fellow operators on the same side will likely
have the same difficulty. As the coater machine
operators finish each mill roll (which their machine
has slit into a batch of machine rolls), they label
it. When one batch is depleted, the material handlers are supposed to select the next oldest coated
batch. If a batch looks like it is going to be
waxy to them, they frequently try to avoid conflicts
with their machine operators by switching the labels
between batches. This way they get to use what
appears to be a better batch, and the waxy batch is
left for the next shift to cope with. This coping
mechanism is one aspect of a fairly pervasive
"shiftism" in the department.

Occasionally there are other paper defects that
arise not from the coating operation but from malfunctions in the paper-making process at the paper
mill. These defects -- holes or breaks in the
paper, uneven tension across the roll -- when they
occur, are certain to cause jam-ups for the operators. These defects, however, are rare experiences
for operators, since such paper will have normally
jammed the coating machine first and have been discarded by the coating machine operators. Since this
occurs so rarely, machine operators have not developed any working knowledge about these defects.
Operators appear to think of them fatalistically, as
being outside of their control, while they feel they
can at least partially predict and control the more
common coating defects.

Knowledge about the machinery. The hundreds of
individual items of knowledge about their machinery
that operators described and presented in their
interviews fall into four broad categories: knowledge about the specific characteristics of individual machines that effect speed capability; knowledge about certain adjustment and repair procedures
that are nominally a part of the mechanics' job;
knowledge about non-standard ways of modifying the
machine to make adjustment in areas that the
machines' designers and engineers had not thought of
and provided for; knowledge about unsanctioned
methods of cleaning certain parts of the machine
while it is still running. Although all of this
working knowledge contributes directly to production by enhancing the women's ability to keep the
machine running and to avoid defects, none of this
knowledge is a part of the company's formal expectations for the machine operating job. The company

49

expects operators to avoid defects and keep their machines operating. The machine knowledge discussed here allows operators to go a long step beyond that. They not only recognize defects, but they learn to diagnose and eliminate their causes; they not only run the machines, but they predict and control the causes of machine stoppages.

More than any other single attribute, the machine operators agreed that, to be good, an operator must "know her machine." Over and over again, operators use the analogy between operating one of their machines and driving a car.

> Cars are basically the same, but every car is different....At first when you're learning, you just learn rules about driving. But as you get to know how to drive, you get a feel for the car you're driving -- you know, things like how it feels at different speeds, how well the brakes work, when it's going to overheat, how to start it when it's cold.... Then if you think about old cars like these machines, been running three shifts for twenty years, some of them, like maybe you've got a car with no horn, that wants to turn right when you hit the brake, that don't start right unless you pump the gas a special way -- then maybe you can start to see what it's like trying to run those junky old machines they've got down there.... Now a good operator is like when you put her on a new machine she knows these machines so well, she's got a feel for it, she picks up right away what she's got to do different on this new machine than she was doing on the other one.*

Although one operator developed this analogy in greater detail, others also used it. The main point that they were all trying to make is that it is not enough just to know how to start, stop, clean and maintain these machines. That level of knowledge -- knowing the "rules about driving" -- is about the

---

*It is important to note that the machinery in the department is neither unusually old nor obsolete. It is "state of the art" in the industry, and it is newer than the median age of capital equipment in manufacturing. (See Melman, 1965).

level that the women reach by the end of their
three-day training period. The next higher level of
knowledgeability, which is the real sine qua non
of successful machine operation, requires that the
operators learn the idiosyncrasies of their individual machines. Several operators noted that if
these machines are to be run right (that is, without continually encountering breakdowns and defects
that are normally avoidable) they must be "babied."
Babying a machine involves a process of learning
the machine's peculiar idiosyncrasies and adjusting
one's mode of operation accordingly. This level of
knowledgeability and machine sensitivity is expected
of each operator by her fellow operators and other
workers in the department. Management, however,
has no such expectations and gives no evidence of
even being aware of these subtleties. Women who are
acknowledged to be especially "good" operators
develop a "feel" for the machinery that goes beyond
even this level of knowledgeability.

A few examples of the kinds of things the
operators talk about when they describe their
machines and their individual differences will show
the depth of knowledge about the machines that
operators must possess. One of the crucial ways
that these machines all differ from each other is
in their potential maximum feasible speed of operation and in their speed regulation mechanisms.
According to a mechanic interviewed, the timing
mechanisms of these machines (that is, the mechanical linkages that synchronize the different operations of the machine) are considerably worn down.
Each machine varies slightly in the degree of wear
of its individual parts. This important factor
determines how fast a particular may be operated
without "going out of sync" and jamming. Through
careful observation and a certain unavoidable
residual amount of trial and error, an operator
can determine how fast a machine can be run (given
a certain level of paper, glue, and ink quality)
and still put out qualitatively acceptable products.

This process of determining the appropriate
maximum speed, difficult enough in itself, is made
even harder by the deteriorated condition of the
speed-regulation mechanism. Each machine has a
speed adjustment dial. If equipped with an edger,
as are all of the "light" and most of the "heavy"
machines, there is a separate identical dial. There
are numerical markings on all of these dials, which
presumably corresponded to some objective indicator
of machine speed, but the long cycle of wear and

51

partial repair over the years has severed any connection between these dial markings and actual machine speed. A dial setting of 60 on one machine is a faster or slower speed than the same dial setting on any other machine. Even the edger must be set on a nominally different speed level to get it to synchronize with the rest of the machine. Thus there is no inter-machine, or even intra-machine, reliability in the dials, although each dial is relatively consistent over time.

Other types of machine adjustments that are possible have already been suggested in the previous section describing how machine operators compensate for bad paper. Some of these adjustments involve moving knobs or machine parts by hand, but most require specialized tools. Usually an improvised tool can be found, for example, using a scraper-blade instead of a screw driver, but some operators have acquired different types of allen wrenches and screw drivers used to make these adjustments.*

Since these are multi-function machines, they require an elaborate conveyer system to move the paper from step to step through each stage in the production. Each machine has an array of pressure rollers, paper guides, vacuum nozzles ("titties"), insertors ("peckers"), and mechanical holders ("grabbers"), which are necessary to move the paper at the right time into the right place for the next step in the production process. If the paper is at all misaligned, these mechanisms fail to hold the paper properly, and a jam-up usually results. To avoid jam-ups, operators therefore find ways to adjust these conveyer mechanisms, even those that are unadjustable within the framework of the machine's design. They bend grabbers and flatten paper guides; they put a layer of tape on some surfaces to lessen the vacuum pressure from the titties; they wrap tape around the pecker to stiffen it; they build up paper and tape behind various rubber gaskets to increase their pressure. In these ways they wring high quality production out of machines that are so far removed from their design specifications that technically they shouldn't even be operable.

Sometimes they make "hammer repairs." In the normal course of production, machine parts work out

_____

*Three of the operators interviewed owned and used such tools. All three were included in the group named by operator informants as "good operators."

52

of position -- chipper knives are particularly prone to do this -- and have to be put back where they belong. Mechanics often do this with a small machine hammer; operators use the weights from their balancing scale. This is a touchy procedure. Mechanics who do this too vigorously, or too frequently, or to inappropriate parts get the reputation of being "hammer happy" and are looked down on by the other mechanics. Mechanics expect good operators to use the technique judiciously, that is, to know under what circumstances it is appropriate and under what circumstances a more basic repair is called for.

Operators know machine cleanliness is a crucial key to production quality (and to quantity, since jams and defects slow production). At one point or another in the interview all seven of the operator informants stressed the necessity of machine cleanliness. But they are talking about a highly selective, technically informed concept of cleanliness. Production does not require that these machines sparkle with polish; production does however require that certain critical working parts of the machine be kept free of built-up ink, glue, or paper scraps. If the operator allows these materials to build up, sooner or later the machine will either jam or start to produce defective products. When the machine is running smoothly and everything is going well, this puts the operator in a dilemma. Her basic feeling is that she has a good thing going and she does not want to stop and possibly mess it up. Yet the trouble-making build-up is inexorable. When the machine is running well, it is asking for trouble to stop it -- the glue and ink begin to dry and thicken, the stop and start might throw the print out of register. But not stopping and not cleaning the machine is asking for trouble too.

Operators have been able to partially resolve this recurring dilemma by developing methods of cleaning some critical parts of the machine while the machine is still running. All these methods are at least contrary to safety regulations, and some are plain dangerous, as the operators admit. Build-up occurs most rapidly on rollers in the printing unit. Cleaning them periodically is formally the job of the inkman or his assistant. Many operators clean their own, however, reasoning that by the time they stop the machine and wait for the inkman other problems might develop. If the operator is willing to gamble, these rollers

53

may be cleanred while the machine is still running.
The technique involves wiping the rollers (which
are spinning at several hundred r.p.m.'s) with a
cleaning rag. If any part of the rag is allowed to
wander a fraction of an inch on the roller, it can
become caught between two adjacent spinning rollers,
which instantaneously grab the rag and pull it and
possibly the operator's hands into the machinery.
The operators (and the ink men) have therefore
developed a special technique for holding the rag, a
technique which they feel allows them to hold the
rag firmly while nevertheless being prepared to let
go of it at once. Although all the operators know
that this is extremely dangerous, they do not feel
that it leads to accidents, because:

> When you're doing it that way, you know
> how dangerous it is. It's like you're
> super aware so it's probably really
> safer that way than some of the other
> things you do all the time without
> thinking.

Other cleaning techniques involve waiting for precisely the appropriate point in the machine cycle to
insert a long cardboard prod, taped together out of
a piece of packing box, into the machine to dis-
lodge large pieces of paper scraps that might potentially cause a jam. This is also dangerous, but
less so than the roller cleaning operation.* Although the advantages of these cleaning techniques
for productivity and worker convenience are obvious,
the comment quoted above and others like it lead me
to suspect that other functions may be served by
these dangerous practices. It is exciting to do
something dangerous -- the hands tense, the heart
beats, and the adrenalin pumps. It breaks up the
more monotonous parts of the day. In addition,
successful completion of each dangerous cleaning

---

*Another safety regulation that is regularly disregarded,
although for different reasons, is the requirement that
operators wear ear plugs. Most operators loosely insert
fluffs of cotton into their outer ears, so that the
appearance of wearing ear plugs is maintained without
impairing the wearer's ability to carry on a shouted conversation with other workers on the floor.

operation reaffirms the workers' own sense of
possessing abilities "above and beyond the call of
duty.*

<u>Knowledge about quality standards.</u> In the
previous section, the various references to the
operators' knowledge of product defects focused on
their diagnoses of the causes of these defects.
Here the emphasis is on the operators' knowledge of
the precise boundaries between acceptable and unacceptable quality. The development of "an eye for
cones" is an extremely important part of the operator's job, emphasized by management and workers
alike. An unusually precise knowledge of the quality standards for each type of defect is repeatedly
mentioned by the operators as a distinguishing
characteristic of a "good" operator.
    Once again, this type of working knowledge in-
volved heightened perceptual acuity. Although
quality judgments regarding some types of defects
involve simple dichotomies, most types of defects
involve judging the product's relative position
along a continuum of quality. Defects of this latter type include all of the possible printing
errors, and "funnels" (pinholes in the tips of the
cones). In these defects the differences between
acceptable and unacceptable quality are so slight
that they are invisible to the outsider. Operators
not only develop an ability to see these differences but learn to spot them in a fraction of a
second's time, as each product passes before their
eyes while "bridging" or "tumbling."
    Perceiving small differences is the easiest
part of the quality judging process. The hard
part is knowing, for each different defect's quality continuum, the exact point that separates
acceptable from unacceptable quality. There are
certain rules of thumb that are given to new operators during the training period -- for instance, a
prinz color may be up to 1/16th of an inch out of
register before it should be rejected -- but in
actual operation nobody stops to take micrometer

_____

*Reading this, an operator informant commented, "You
could be right, but I think this is probably bullshit.
You just don't realize what a pain in the ass it is to
shut down and reach all around inside there to clean it."

55

readings. Each operator is expected by management, by the inspectors, and by the other operators, to just "know" what the quality standard is. Each individual operator develops her own standards, but the system of frequent checks by the quality control inspectors insures that the operator's standards will conform very closely to those of the inspectors. The operator may, however, set standards that are higher than the inspectors'. Most of the operators interviewed said that they did this, at least for some types of defects.

> If you're not careful, you can get to be a fanatic about these things really..... It gets so bad that I can't even go into a store without going over.... and checking the print on the (brand-name item packed in cones).... People talk all the time about how they like to pack good cones. It feels good when everything's going right and the cones are coming out perfectly.... You want it to be right. Even when management doesn't care, and the customer wouldn't notice, I would be concerned about it.

While the inspection system assures that operators' standards will be no lower than the inspectors', they may well be higher. A similar sort of relation also exists between the inspectors and management. According to several of the operators, including one former inspector, the inspectors set standards that are higher than management's. When the inspectors find too many defective cups in an operator's packing case, she "tags the case." These tagged cases are set aside. When the relief operators are not actually relieving somebody, they sort through these tagged cases, separating acceptable from unacceptable cones, a process that is known as "picking cones." Occasionally Prezzi or Blum will check up on this operation, look at a few of the cones that are being rejected, and arbitrarily decide that the whole case is "good enough." Management sometimes tries other ways to get the operators to lower their standards.

> Every two months or so Prezzi gives a speech to the operators and tells us to be sure not to throw out cups that are good enough. He talks about paper shortage

and ecology and all that, but what he is
really talking about is the company's
profit. But it doesn't change anything,
because inspectors' standards don't
change.

As Watson has pointed out (1971) this kind of
tension between the managers (who are expected to
keep costs down and productivity up) and the workers
(who are expected to produce good quality products)
is endemic to capitalist production. In Marxist
terms, it is but one of the many manifestations of
the contradiction between concrete and abstract
labor, between the production of useful goods ("use
values") and saleable goods ("exchange values").
Operators' working knowledge about quality
standards is more complex than might at first be
apparent. They need to know both product parameters
and standards of the inspectors on their shift.
Since these are not critical products, the quality
standards on all parameters bear little relation to
the actual usability of the product for the ultimate
consumer. In other words, many of the rejected
products could still serve as perfectly adequate
food containers. There is therefore no finally
determining reference point upon which these quality
standards can be based. Standards vary informally,
but significantly, from shift to shift, depending
on the consensus that each shift's inspectors work
out among themselves. For instance, since cones
are used to hold liquids, no funnels are permitted
on the "heavy" side no matter how small the pinhole.
There is no similar functional requirement on the
"light" side, however, and small pinholes are therefore acceptable to the inspectors and operators on
the second shift, but not on the first. This is
exactly analogous to the situation in major league
baseball, where it is well known that the umpires
in the American League and the National League apply
subtly different standards in calling balls and
strikes. Being transferred from one shift to
another is like being traded from one league in
baseball to another: it takes a little while to
adjust to the different standards being applied in
the new league.
The lack of correspondence between department
workers' standards and the useability standards of
the consumer creates ambivalence toward these
quality standards on the part of the operators. On
the one hand, they respect and internalize the in-

spectors' standards. An operator's ability to dis-
cern these standards and perform up to them is a
source of respect from her fellow operators. Within
the work community, the standards are legitimate.
On the other hand, the overriding concern of the
shift leader and the other mechanics with "production responsibility" is quantity, not quality.
Operators are aware that many of the cones that they
reject would actually be perfectly acceptable to the
customer. Almost all operators in the department
therefore engage in a practice of separating out
the cones that are substandard but still usable.
They hide these around, and they wait for an inspector to pass by and approve a case before they
pull these out of hiding and pack them.

There thus exists in the operators' work community two distinct sets of quality standards, both
of which are legitimate. The standard of presentation is the standard that is applied within the work
community. Operators take care to demonstrate to
the inspectors and to each other that they know
what these standards are and that they can consistently present to the inspectors cases of cones
that meet these standards. There also exists a
standard of usability that operators use in deciding
which cones are acceptable to ship to the customers
and consumers outside the work community. The
standard of presentation reflects pride in workmanship and transforms the production of the humble but
useful products into an end in itself. The standard
of useability reflects the operators' realization
that in the world outside of the work community,
these products are not ends in themselves but only
means toward other ends, namely the marketing and
consumption of the food products which these cones
will eventually contain.

Knowledge about the work community. Workers'
cooperative face-to-face interaction is a technical
necessity of production, required by the particular
form of the organization of production and division
of labor. As in any other type of community, workers use this base of formally required cooperative
association to build a complex network of informal
forms of sociability. To the superficial observer
these may appear quite frivolous, but they are not.
They are the mechanisms by which workers nurture
the relations of trust and cooperation that are
necessary to production.

Their nurturance of relations of trust and
cooperation is necessary for the maintenance of

58

productivity in the cone department as a whole, but
it is also necessary for the productivity of individual workers. Interviews with cone department
workers revealed that at least on some levels their
cultivation of informal relations is quite consciously instrumental in intent. One woman called
this "survival knowledge," knowing how to cultivate
the kinds of relations with fellow workers that will
assure that their assistance and cooperation will be
forthcoming when needed.

Workers in the cone department put a lot of
time and effort into a constant process of nurtur-
ing these informal relations. This is mostly, one
imagines, because it is a humane, pleasant, and rewarding way of passing the time, but it is at least
partially also because such constant attention is
necessary to overcome the competitive and antagon-
istic tendencies that are fostered by the department's division of labor. In the long run, it is
absolutely necessary that operators, material handlers, mechanics, and inkmen all cooperate with
each other; but in the short run individual inter-
group interactions are almost always potential
sources of conflict.* The mechanic is already
working on something, but if he does not come over
to make a minor repair on a particular machine right
away, all glue and ink on the machine are going to
dry up and that machine's operator is going to have
to scrape and clean the whole machine completely
before she can start it up again. The material
handler is on a break, but the operator's machine
is out of paper. The workers in these situations
need to have built up a stock of feelings of good
will and cooperativeness that they can draw upon to
negotiate these potential conflicts. Building up
this stock of good will involves a myriad of social
activities. Workers bring in snapshots of their
family activities and show them around. They bring
in food and throw small parties to celebrate birth-
days and other personal events. On the night
shifts they also bring in liquor, usually vodka,
kept hidden in the lockers and dispensed into the

---

*Because these constant small conflicts have a high saliance
for the outside observer, it takes a kind of Simmelian
imagination to see the dialectical manner in which such conflict implies an underlying cooperation. Communities are co-
hesive, more solidary than fragmentary, but this only implies
the ultimate subordination of conflict, not its complete
absence.

soft drinks which people sip while they work. They
make handicraft items and sell them to each other,
or they sell each other products from Tupperware,
Amway, Avon and the like. Workers convert the
sexual division of labor, with its constant underlying tension, into a source of humor and pleasant
flirtatiousness. (Often more than just flirtatiousness is involved -- the department contains
many dating relationships and several extra-marital
affairs.) To a lesser extent, the potential racial
tensions are also used as material for humorous by-
play. All of these activities contribute to the
social atmosphere of the department, which workers
find very pleasant. All but two of the workers
interviewed cited the other people in the work
community as "the best thing about the job."*
There just is not space, however, to describe these
activities in the kind of detail that folklorists
and others would appreciate. Instead, the discussion here will focus on the types of interaction
patterns that machine operators themselves see as
instrumentally necessary to the successful performance of their jobs.

For machine operators the most important goal
of their interpersonal relations is to secure the
cooperation of the mechanics, inkmen, material
handlers, and other operators on their side. Since
all those people (except the other operators, whose
cooperation is less necessary though still important) are likely to be men, some operators rely on
"feminine wiles" to get their cooperation. Most
operators, however, to a greater or lesser extent
supplement this basic technique with another
strategy. They try to acquire and maintain the
reputation of being "a good operator." This image
of competence is crucial, because if they can maintain it, it lends credibility to the claims and
requests that they make of other workers. If an
operator whom he believes is competent asks for
help, the mechanic is much more likely to accept
her representations that: (a) there really is
something wrong with the machine that could not be
fixed with a routine cleaning; and (b) whatever is
wrong is unavoidably wrong (that is, it was not
caused by operator negligence), and therefore her
problem is more "deserving" of his attention. In a
similar fashion, the image of competence eases the

---

*The other two responses were: "It's my second home", and
"It's a living, an honest living."

60

claims for service that she might have to make on inkmen and material handlers. If other operators on her side also perceive an operator as being competent, they are more likely to agree to join her in the informal mutual-aid arrangements that operators often make to ease their work. The most common of these informal arrangements is "to go five by five," the cone department's version of the "doubling up" arrangement that workers often use in assembly line situations. When two workers "go five by five" with each other, they agree that each will run two machines for "five minutes" (Actually ten to fifteen minutes is the more usual length of time.) while the other operator takes an extra break. Operators will normally only make such mutual agreements if each perceives that the other is a good enough operator to be able to operate two machines at once and to get her machine "set up," that is, properly cleaned and adjusted, so that it can run trouble-free at least until the "five-by-five" is over.

In addition, an operator who is having trouble with her machine can count on advice and sympathetic hearing from the other more experienced operators on her side only if she has an image of competence. According to one of the more experienced operators interviewed,

> If she is one of the ones that's always having trouble anyway, I probably wouldn't bother to try and help. There's probably so many things out of whack on her machine anyway, any advice you could give probably wouldn't help much anyway.

For machine operators in the cone department, it is of much more practical importance that her fellow workers accept her image of competence than it is that management do so. Since management rarely hassles any operators anyway (no negative sanctions), and since there are no merit promotions or raises for operators (no positive sanctions), whatever image of competence that management has of a particular operator is not as likely to affect her daily life as her fellow workers' attitudes are.

Although it is not possible to cover all of the machine operators' working knowledge in this brief sketch, the purpose has been to present enough examples to indicate the breadth and extent of the knowledge. The machinery, the materials, and the organizational relations of production are all complex subject areas that the operators must learn in detail in order to do their jobs. Knowledge of all these areas is a technical necessity of production, because the operators do not merely passively tend their machines. They actively keep their machines running, meeting and successfully overcoming all the material and social obstacles which periodically arise to interfere with continued quality production.

3. The Newton Branch of the Arnold National Bank

Newton is a recent development located at the outer fringe of the area of suburban sprawl that has developed since World War II around one of the major metropolitan centers in the eastern United States. Larger in scale than most such developments; it has better recreation facilities, more pools and tennis courts. Although it has several light industrial plants and large office buildings, most of the people that work there do not live in Newton, while most of the people who live in Newton commute to work elsewhere. The price levels of homes and apartments, both for sale and rent, have risen so rapidly in the last six years that only people with above average incomes can afford to buy or even rent in Newton.

Newton has proven to be a successful concept in residential marketing. It is an attractive enough development so that would-be suburbanites are willing to pay a slight premium over the cost of comparable housing in other areas to buy or rent in Newton. The developers of Newton, a subsidiary of a large multi-national corporation, have found it to be a financially rewarding project.

The metropolitan area that includes Newton enjoys a relatively healthy, expanding economic base, and the Newton area is one of the two most rapidly expanding market areas in this region. The population of the area is growing rapidly, and the newcomers are relatively affluent. For all these reasons, national and local retail chains are scrambling to get themselves established in this market. The competition has led to a phenomenon of pre-emptive siting. Chains that can afford to take a temporary loss will open up an outlet in this market area before the population in the area has reached a large enough size to provide a profitable

volume of trade. For the chains which are large
enough to afford such a temporary loss, pre-emptive
siting is a worth-while competitive technique to
capture new markets. The large number of branch
banks in Newton is a reflection of the banks' use
of this technique.

The Arnold National Bank. The Arnold National
Bank is a commercial bank founded about ten years
ago by a consortium of local businessmen to serve
the expanding suburban market in the counties
directly to the west of the central city. The ex-
plosive suburban growth of these counties in the
early '60's led to the formation of at least a half
dozen new suburban commercial banks. Although some
of these new banks remain marginal operations today,
Arnold has prospered and expanded into a medium size
multi-branch operation, although still much smaller
than the established national banks downtown.

While Arnold has undergone a relatively rapid
expansion, its growth has not been smooth or un-
troubled. There have been splits and disagreements
among the original founders which were reflected in
a rapid turnover of top management personnel and an
unsettled atmosphere in the bank generally. All of
these problems were resolved when the bank was taken
over two years before the study by a state-wide
bank holding company. Under the new ownership, a
new top management team has been able to open new
branches and expand old ones, streamline accounting
procedures with new computer facilities and programs
that have increased efficiency to a level more in
line with accepted large-bank standards in the industry, and reduce the number of full time employees
from 125 to 75. At present, the bank now has seven
branches (including the main office) and total
assets of around $35 million.

The Newton Branch. Since it first opened a
little over three years ago, the Newton branch
has become Arnold National's largest and most
successful branch bank. Its five office windows
and two drive-up windows serve about 5,000 accounts.
This is more customers than a bank this size can
comfortably handle, and in the past year the Arnold
National Bank has responded to this problem by
opening another branch in North Newton and by building an addition, now under construction, that will
provide three additional walk-up and drive-up teller stations.

Employees at the branch take pride in this
record of success and are generally proud to be a
part of the "best branch" of the bank. Despite the
relatively high workload, morale is high. Compared
to other banks in the area, the Newton branch maintains a "friendly atmosphere" which is immediately
perceptible on entering the building. This is partly due to the architectural arrangements -- carpet-
ing on the floor and a minimal use of bullet-proof
glass to separate the customers from the employees.
It is partly due to the special accommodations provided in the lobby for bank customers -- comfortable
lounge chairs, a coffee tables, a coffee machine
that provides free coffee. It is also partly due to
the "friendliness" of the tellers, a combination of
genuine personal pleasantness and learned techniques
which are described below.

Customers regularly tell the tellers how much
they appreciate the friendliness of the Newton
branch in comparison to both other banks in Newton
and other branches of the Arnold Bank. The warm
atmosphere is quite palpable -- there is a striking
difference between this branch and the dozen other
branch banks that I have observed in the same metropolitan area. Tellers, therefore, tend to attribute
the success of the branch primarily to this difference in atmosphere, a perception that is reinforced
both by customers and the branch management. Nevertheless, the branch's growth is at least as likely
to be explained by its excellent location. Newton
is in the center of the fastest growing suburban
area in the southern counties, and the branch is
located in the busiest shopping center in Newton.
Although it has about the same number of stores,
the new shopping center in North Newton, for instance, appears almost dead by comparison.

Aside from Arnold National's two branches, two
other commercial banks have opened branches in Newton, as have two savings and loan associations.
Arnold's Newton branch is the biggest, busiest, and
best located of any of these establishments. One of
the savings and loan branches is in the same shopping center as the Arnold branch, but as might be
expected, it is a much smaller operation than the
commercial bank.

An Introduction to Commercial Banking

In advertising campaigns over the last ten
years or so, many commercial banks have called themselves "Full Service Banks" in implied contrast to

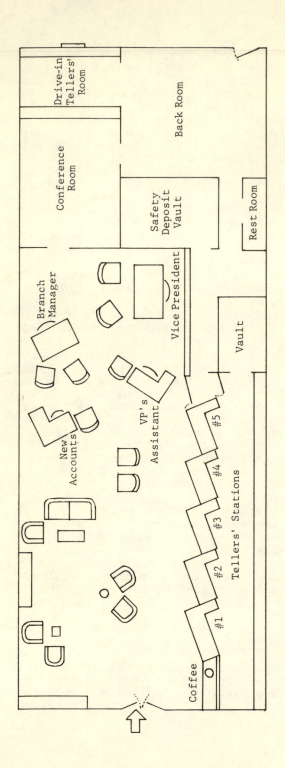

Floor Plan, Newton Branch of the Arnold National Bank

other savings institutions. It is true that commercial banks do offer a wide range of banking services, including many that go beyond the traditional role of savings depository and loan source. Through its employees, the Arnold National Bank is prepared to offer all of the following services: checking accounts (business and personal), savings accounts, certificates of deposit, Christmas Club accounts, several different types of commercial and personal loans, safe deposit boxes, Travelers Checks, Money Orders, cashier's checks, certified checks, letters of credit, redemption of food stamps, receipt of BankAmericard and Master Charge credits from merchants, sale and redemption of U.S. Treasury bills and Savings Bonds, sale and purchase of stocks, collection of commercial paper, and preparation of business payrolls.

These services are so varied that people in the bank group them into the general category of "customer transactions". This word is used to describe any interaction between the customer and the bank. When customers want to use one of the bank's services -- for instance, if they want to cash a check or redeem a savings bond -- they must approach a teller (or for some services, a bank official) to make the transaction. Tellers will make the exchange and fill out the proper form to initiate the recording of the transaction in the bank's books.

Most of these transactions involve the exchange of the bank's principal commodity, that is money, either in the form of actual cash or some type of credit instrument. Money is valuable -- in fact, that is all it is, a symbolic representation of condensed value, and such credit instruments as checks are even more symbolic, more condensed, and more valuable. It is thus an everyday part of the bankers' experience that very simple transactions can effect the exchange of large sums. Accordingly, these transactions are made very cautiously, and the procedures for each transaction includes several safeguards to ensure the accuracy of the exchange. A second consequence of the condensed value of money is that banks are convenient sources from which to steal relatively large sums of money. Robberies occur often enough -- the Newton branch was robbed about six months ago -- so that bank employees are constantly "security conscious." Employees are also used to having their work scrutinized by various federal, state and internal auditors.

The Formal Organization Of The Newton Branch

   Thirteen people work at the Newton branch: a
bank vice president, his assistant, the branch
manager, the new accounts desk person, the head
teller, four full time tellers, and four part time
tellers. All the employees except for the vice
president are women. The women are basically strat-
ified into "tellers" and "desk people." All the
desk people started out as tellers -- eight, six,
and four years ago, respectively. The head teller
has worked for the bank two and a half years; the
other tellers have all worked there two years or
less.
   Mr. Davis is the Executive Vice President of
the Arnold National Bank. As such, he is in charge
of, among many other things, the operation of all
branches. His is the third highest position in the
bank's hierarchy. Until the holding company took
over, his was the second highest position, but the
holding company added another man over him. Shortly
after the takeover, he moved out of the main office
to the Newton branch, bringing with him Therese, the
new branch manager, and hiring Elizabeth to fill the
newly-created position of his assistant. Before Mr.
Davis arrived, the Newton branch had gone through
three branch managers in a little over two years
and existed in a generalized state of unmanaged
chaos, a problem which presently afflicts the new
North Newton branch and which is apparently the
normal situation of new Arnold branches when they
first open up. When Mr. Davis arrived, he completly
reorganized the branch. In addition to the new
manager and his new assistant, the two most senior
tellers were promoted to the new accounts desk and
to the head teller's position. New tellers were
hired, and all but one of these have stayed with the
bank. Partly as a result of these moves, and partly
as a result of tellers' own initiatives which will
be discussed later, the people at the Newton branch
now work at higher levels of both morale and productivity than before.
   Mr. Davis' assistant holds a unique position in
the Arnold Bank. She refers to her position as
"Assistant Branch Manager" but nobody else interviewed seems to have heard of this title; they refer
to her as "Mr. Davis' assistant" or "Mr. Davis'
secretary." Her job functions are relatively unspecified -- nobody every told her exactly what she

is supposed to do -- and she has expanded the responsibilities of the job as much as possible. Besides taking care of Mr. Davis' correspondence, she
is in charge of checking people in and out of the
safety deposit box area. She interviews applicants
for small loans, but she does not "have a signature
with the bank" (that is, she is not authorized to
approve or reject loans), so she can only make
recommendations to Mr. Davis or to Therese, the
branch manager. She also "comes in early every
morning to open up and check out everything and make
sure it's secure," and she has taken on the job of
calling the overdrawn customers -- about twenty per
day -- to tell them to come in and make a deposit.

     The branch manager's job involves an overall
responsibility for the smooth operation of the
branch. She hires, schedules, and evaluates all of
the branch's personnel. She has a "signature" which
means that she (or Mr. Davis) must personally
approve any large or unusual transaction before it
takes place. Much of her work is in the area of
customer relations: taking loan applications, dealing personally with important customers, straightening out complaints and grievances. She is responsible for the maintenance of security and for the
general carrying out of Arnold Bank policies in the
Newton branch.

     In actual practice, whenever Mr. Davis is pres-
ent, which is most of the time, he also shares all
of the functions and responsibilities that are normally a part of the branch manager's job. According to the desk people interviewed, he seems to prefer this "less important" work, especially the dealing with individual customers, over his other administrative responsibilities. Although this overlap
of responsibilities would appear to be a potential
source of conflict, the interviews indicate that Mr.
Davis and Therese generally operate as a team, just
as they apparently did before they came to Newton.
Much of this overlap is inevitable since Mr. Davis
is specifically responsible for the operation of
all branches and Newton is the largest branch. From
the perspective of the employees, when they need input from management, they might go to whichever one
of the two is not busy. Although they respect Mr.
Davis, they clearly prefer to deal with Therese
because she is friendlier and more informal. (For
example, none of the employees call Mr. Davis by his
first name or Therese by her second.)

     At the new accounts desk, the other "desk per-
son" greets new customers and helps them open their

accounts, serves as an informal receptionist for customers who want to talk to other desk people, answers the telephone, helps customers who have problems with their accounts, handles the new accounts paperwork, prepares four or five reports a week on such subjects as savings bonds sold and new accounts opened, and helps with some of Mr. Davis' typing. The job thus involves a combination of customer service tasks, which cannot be scheduled in advance and must be taken on whenever customers happen to come in, and other paperwork tasks that must be handled between customers.

The highest ranking person on the bank who is responsible for the handling of actual cash is the head teller. She is the guardian of the vault, monitoring and signing off on anything that goes in or out. She is also responsible for the money handled by the other tellers. At the end of the day she writes up the branch settlement, which requires her to check out and sum up all of the individual settlements of each teller. She also compiles the daily reports on the amount of money orders and Travelers Checks sold. She keeps track of the amount of cash and coin in the branch, and decides when it is necessary to ship some out or order more in. She prepares the money for shipment, and she supervises the verification of the amounts received. Tellers feel that the head teller does "four times the work of anybody else in the bank." In addition to the duties already described the head teller has her own window and handles customer transactions like all the other tellers. Although the head teller has a lot of direct responsibility, she is perceived by other bank workers, both tellers and desk people, as still basically "just a teller." Before the woman who now works on new accounts was promoted from a teller's position, she was given her choice between the new accounts desk and the head teller's job. "Even though the head teller is a more important job probably," she chose the desk job because "the management doesn't really notice the tellers, but they come in contact with people that work on the desk.... On desk there is a chance for advancement."

Tellers handle the routine transactions between the bank and its customers. They cash checks, take deposits, sell money orders -- taking in cash, handing it out, and counting it twice each time they touch it. They keep a running record of all their "ins" and "outs". Each transaction usually involves shifting cash in or out of their money drawer;

collecting checks, receipts or other paper that indicates where money went in a bin called the "works"; putting each transaction onto an adding machine tape; and writing each one down on a lined pad. The works bin, the adding machine tape, and the entries on the pad are all necessary to enable the teller to "settle up" or balance out at the end of the day. In addition to "operating" her window, the tellers must also draw up daily reports on Master Charge and BankAmericard payouts, food stamp redemptions, bond sales, utility bill payments received, installment loan payments received, and Christmas Club deposits. The "food stamp teller" handles the food stamp report regularly, but all the other reports are rotated on a weekly basis, an arrangement worked out by the tellers themselves. Before the tellers made this arrangement, these reports were not assigned and written up until after the bank closed at 2 o'clock. Now, the tellers all know which reports they are responsible for and they can compile them gradually throughout the day. Under this new system, if they don't have any problems settling up, tellers can usually leave the bank by 2:30 or 2:45 in the afternoon, almost an hour earlier than was previously possible.

Working time and working shifts. The bank is open from 9:00 A.M. until 2:00 P.M. every day of the week. On Fridays, it reopens again from 5:00 P.M. until 8:00 P.M., and it is open Saturday morning from 9:00 A.M. until 12 noon. The drive-in windows are open from 8:00 A.M. to 8:00 P.M., Monday through Friday. Full time tellers come to work at 8:30 in the morning.* Tellers are free to leave at whatever time they finish settling up at the end of the day, usually around 2:30 or 3:00 in the afternoon. These are very convenient hours for women with school-age children, a positive aspect of the job that was pointed out by all the tellers interviewed. In addition to these regular hours, everybody in the bank, from Mr. Davis on down, also works about eight extra hours on Friday night and Saturday of alternate weekends. Since they have a half-hour lunch break for which they are required to punch out, the average work week for tellers is around twenty-seven

---

*They start a half hour earlier on Mondays, because of the extra backlog of work collected in the "night depository" over the weekend.

and one-half hours on their off weeks, around thirty-five and a half hours when they work week-ends.

Thus, tellers whom the bank considers to be "full time" are not really working the number of hours that would be considered full time on most other jobs. The distinction between full time and part time tellers at the bank does not refer to the number of hours worked, but rather to the basis of their salary. Full time people are paid by the week, part time people by the hour. At the Arnold Bank, some of the part time tellers work almost as many hours as the full time tellers, and earn approximately the same pay. Part time tellers do most of the work on the drive-in windows. They also work weekends, and come in to replace full time tellers who are absent.

The bank has a time clock in the back room, and everybody below the branch manager punches in and out. Although only part time tellers are paid on the basis of actual hours worked, the bank is quite serious about punching the time. Employees take the time clock seriously, trying hard to get in on time in the morning and making sure that they do not take more than any half hour for lunch. As one of the tellers noted in her interview, nobody every punches each other in or out, although this was a common practice in places she had previously worked.

Another reason why the tellers are careful not to let their lunch break run long is the tightly scheduled system for taking these breaks. The lunch hour is one of the peak periods of customer traffic during the day. Only one teller can take her lunch break at a time, therefore, since it is not practical to shut down more than one teller's window at once. One after the other, the five tellers must take their lunch breaks, and this in an office that closes at two. There is no slack in the schedule; if anybody runs over, the last person is going to be cheated out of a part of her break.

Other than the lunch break, there are no other officially sanctioned "coffee breaks" during the day. The work day is short enough so that most tellers don't feel any need for this, anyway. At the Newton branch, the employees are free to help themselves to the customers' free coffee in the lobby. Most workers have their own mugs at their work stations, and intermittently sip coffee throughout the day. This practice is not permitted at other branches of the Arnold Bank, because the

72

inevitable occasional spills can ruin a teller's
"works", a catastrophe that could take hours to
straighten out.

   Pay and incentive systems.   The starting
salary for full time tellers is $95.00 per week.
On the basis of the average number of hours worked
per week (including alternate weekends), this salary
is a little over the equivalent of the Federal minimum wage. Because the job requires only a high
school education with no other specialized training
or previous experience, the tellers interviewed felt
that this wage rate was in line with the other jobs
available in the Newton area for women without
specialized job skills. In general, tellers felt
that the hours and working conditions were good
enough to make this a very desirable job, despite
the pay, which was only adequate. There are more
women with school-age children in Newton looking for
jobs than there are jobs available with such convenient hours. The tellers interviewed who did
have children felt themselves generally lucky to
have found their jobs.
   The starting pay rate for part time tellers is
$3.00 per hour. This is fifty cents per hour over
the going rate for part time retail clerks in the
Newton area, which is almost the only other part
time job available to Newton women. It is also
higher than the equivalent hourly rate for full time
tellers. The one "part time" teller who regularly
works a 40-hour, 6-day week earns significantly
more than the full time tellers. Other part time
tellers also occasionally work 25 or 30 hours per
week, and thus earn approximately the same pay as
the full time people. When they compare their
pay rate with the other jobs that they might have
taken, or with the wages earned by their full time
colleagues, the part time tellers feel that the pay
is pretty good. They do point out, however, that
as part time people they are excluded from the
fringe benefits -- paid holdiays, paid vacations,
medical insurance -- that the full time employees
are entitled to.
   The bank has a system of evaluating each
employee on a quarterly basis. Normally, through
the first year or so on the job these evaluations
result in slight raises in pay. The "regular" pay
rate for tellers, though, is not much higher than
the starting rate. After the first few raises,
tellers do not receive additional pay increases no

73

matter how much "merit" they continue to exhibit.
Other than these quarterly evaluations, the bank has
no other regular formal incentive system for its
employees, not even a procedure for rewarding suggestions.

The bank's "quality control" system; the
constant process of checking for accuracy. At the
tellers' windows, high quality work means work that
is verified accurate, speedy, and friendly. The
bank has procedures to check on all three aspects of
quality, but almost all of its quality control
efforts are spent on maintaining precise accuracy.
The tellers' workday activities and consciousness
are dominated by the necessity of settling out at
the end of the day. Basically, this procedure involves careful tallies of the cash and coin on hand,
the records of the money handed out (the "outs"),
and the money taken in (the "ins"), and the comparison of today's cash on hand with yesterday's to
ensure that every penny of the difference can be
accounted for.*
Verification of accuracy is repeated on three
levels. The first level involved the teller's own
settlement, and the steps she takes during the day
to make sure that she will settle. Next, the head
teller rechecks all these figures with her own
branch settlement. And finally, the bookkeeping
department rechecks all individual transactions,
each teller's settlement, and the branch settlements
as a whole. As they work through the day, tellers
routinely take two kinds of precautions to assure
that they will settle out at the day's end. First
of all, every time money is handled it is normative-
ly counted three times. When a teller disburses
money to a customer, she counts the money when she
takes it out of the money drawer, once again in
front of the window, and a third time as she passes
it to the customer. Money received from customers
is counted twice, first when it is received from
the customer and then as it is put away in the
drawer. Money given to another teller is counted
twice; the receiving teller counts it the third.
All money put into the vault must be counted and
signed off by two different tellers. During the
settling out procedure itself, everything is counted

_____

*The settling up procedure is described in more detail
below.

74

and added twice. Besides verifying every transaction twice, tellers also maintain an informal
record keeping system which records memory-jogging
details of each transaction. This informal record,
which is in addition to the formally required receipts and records that are accumulated in the works
bin is kept "just in case" the settlement does not
come out properly. Should that happen, the informal
record will help the teller to track down which
transaction is the source of the error.

The tellers' settlements are rechecked by the
head teller at the time when she makes out the daily
branch settlement. Both the individual settlements
and the branch settlements are forwarded to the
bookkeeping department which verifies all of them in
detail before proceeding to post the recorded transactions into the customers' accounts. The system of
periodic audits -- by the bank's own auditing department and by the state and federal banking
authorities -- acts as a further check on accuracy.
The emphasis of these audits on the enforcement of
banking regulations and the maintenance of security
against theft and embezzlement means that these
audits do not normally affect the work activities
of individual tellers.

In addition to the system of controlling for
accuracy, periodic checks are also made on the
speed and efficiency of tellers. Tellers are aware
that Mr. Davis and Therese can and do time the duration of individual transactions. The work desks of
both managers are so located that this can be done
unobtrusively. At the Arnold National Bank there is
no systematic method of monitoring the courtesy,
the friendliness or the personalizing techniques of
individual tellers. All have heard about the way
other banks send in inspectors to pose as customers
and observe the tellers as they carried out the
pseudo customer's requests, but they report that
this is not done at Arnold National.

The Bank Teller's Working Knowledge

To do her job satisfactorily, there are about
seventy-five different sets of procedures that the
teller must know how to handle. Each procedure set
consists of number of different actions that the
teller must perform to complete the procedure in
accordance with established bank policy. Around
fifty of these procedure sets involve different
types of transactions between tellers and customers,

or in a few cases, among the tellers themselves. Other procedure sets, such as the daily settlement and the other daily reports, must be carried out each day to meet bookkeeping requirements.

Procedures for handling transactions. In general, any customer transaction requires the teller to: (1) size up the customer, checking out the identity and making sure the account has sufficient funds to support the desired transaction; (2) physically carry out the customer's request (e.g., receive the cash and make out the money order); (3) make out a receipt or other record of the transaction for the customer; (4) record the transaction on the appropriate form for the bookkeeping department; and (5) enter the important elements of the transaction on the teller's own daily record that she uses in the settling process. Although all of the possible types of customer transactions have procedural sets that contain these five elements, the specific procedures to follow are different in each type of transaction, even if the differences are sometimes only slight.

For instance, to cash a check (the most frequently requested type of customer transaction) requires the teller to go through the following procedures. She appraises the check itself -- the date, the written and numbered amounts, the signature. She affirms the identity of the customer, either through her prior personal knowledge, or through a comparison of signatures. If the customer is not known to her, she checks the daily trial balances to make sure that, at least as of the close of the business day yesterday, the account has sufficient funds to cover the check; and she writes the amount of money in the account in pencil on the back of the check to prove that she has in fact checked the trials. If anything so far has raised doubts in her mind about the legitimacy of the check, she sends the customer over to the vice president or to the branch manager to get one of their signatures. (There are several formal and informal guidelines that she follows to spot doubtful checks.) If the check has appeared acceptable, she takes the check, stamps the back of it with her teller's stamp, initials it, and puts it in her "outs" pile in her money drawer. She may record the transaction on her adding machine tape. (Not all tellers do this with simple check-cashing transactions.) Finally, she takes the money out of the drawer, counts it twice, and gives it to the customer.

A straightforward check cashing is the simplest of the customer transactions for the teller to perform. The second most common type of customer transaction is the "split deposit" transaction, in which the customer has a check which he would like to split into a certain amount of cash and a certain amount of deposit to his or her account. A split deposit requires all of the procedures necessary to carry out an ordinary check cashing plus several additional ones. The customer's deposit slip must be initialled and duplicate records of the deposit must be written out, once on the teller's "ins" pad and once on a slip of paper to be put in the "works" bin; a receipt must be prepared for the customer, and the whole transaction must be recorded on the adding machine tape.

The split deposit is an "average" transaction in terms of the amount of work that a teller has to do to complete it. Other types of transactions can be much more time-consuming and involve a much more complex set of required procedures. Of all the types of transactions, the processing of a stop-payment order, the preparation of a certified check, and the sale of Travelers Checks are generally the most burdensome for the teller.

As the customers come and go through the day, the tellers begin to build up collections of the specialized types of transactions that must be compiled separately and reported in daily reports. According to their own informal arrangement, each teller is responsible for one or two of these individual reports every day. Therefore, all day long in the pauses between customers, the tellers "buy" and "sell" these records to each other, so that by the end of the day the food stamp teller, for instance, has acquired the records of all the food stamp redemptions made that day by any other teller in the branch. To effect such an exchange, the seller gathers together all the records from the particular transaction together with any cash taken in. The buyer purchases this material with a receipt in the form of a general ledger credit slip, which the seller puts in her "works" to record the transaction. The buyer puts the money and records away in the same way as she would if she had made the transaction with a customer at her own window.

This system of buying and selling these materials throughout the day saves the tellers considerable time after the bank closes and is a great improvement over the previous method, which was to wait until each teller settled before pulling these materials together and writing up these reports. Formerly, tellers used to also exchange cash and coin of different denominations, a process which they also called buying or selling money. By mutual agreement, however, they no longer do this, because they want to avoid the doubts and suspicions that used to be aroused when a teller, who might have engaged in several such exchanges during the day, cannot settle at the end of the day.

The most complex sets of procedures that tellers must know how to do are the preparation of the daily settlement and the other daily reports required by the bookkeeping department at the end of each work day. The settling-up procedure requires that the teller add up all her "ins" twice, checking to make sure that both adding machine tapes are identical. The "outs" must be added twice in the same way. The cash and coin on hand must be counted and tallied on a special form which has a space for the amount of each denomination. Finally, the cash balance at the opening of the day is added to the "ins" total, the "outs" total is subtracted from this amount, and the resulting figure should be equal to the cash-on-hand count. If everything does not add up right, an event which happens frequently enough to be a constant source of concern, then the teller rechecks all her mathematical calculations. If the error is still not found, then she must go back through all the transactions of the day, looking for the particular transaction which was the source of the error. If she still cannot either settle up or find the source of the error, the head teller is called into the search. If the head teller can't find it, the branch manager or even the executive vice president is called in. This procedure of having the higher-ups in the branch "help" the teller look for her error has the side effect of giving her superiors a precise and accurate picture of what she did during the day and exactly how she did it. This error-searching process, combined with the fact that the branch manager is herself a former teller, means that the bank management has a much more accurate picture of exactly what their employees are doing than seemed to be the case in any other of the work situations studied.

Daily reports are required by the bookkeeping department of all transactions in which the bank actually serves as an agent for some government agency or some other company. Travelers Checks, money orders, Master Charge and BankAmericard credit services, and utility bills are all issued by private companies who pay the bank a commission for handling this business. Likewise, savings bonds and food stamps are issued by different branches of the federal government through commercial banks. In all of these cases, the tellers must total up all the transactions handled by the branch for the particular company or government agency during the day and make out a general ledger credit -- in effect, a deposit slip -- to a special account which the bank has set aside for itself for this purpose. Then she must fill out another form which the bookkeeping department will use as the basis for "withdrawing" the funds from this account, minus the bank's commission, and transmitting them to the appropriate company or government agency.

In addition to all the procedures discussed so far, there are additional sets of procedures that the tellers must follow to ensure that certain security precautions are being taken as the money is handled within the branch itself. In the banking industry, the standard units for the packaging and transporting of money are "straps" and "bags". Paper money is put up in straps, which are packages of one hundred bills (of whatever denomination) held together by paper bands around the middle. Bags are made up of a standardized number of rolls of coins -- the number of rolls in a bag differs with each coin denomination -- which are packaged in cloth bags. All money comes in and out of the bank in straps and bags, and all money in the vault is kept in straps and bags. The reason is obvious -- the only possible way that large quantities of money can be easily counted and handled is if it is packaged in absolutely invariable standardized units. Otherwise, each large money shipment would involve the counting of literally millions of individual bills and coins. Most of the security procedures about the handling of money involve bank policies about the way money should be handled, loose or in straps, when it is held by individual tellers, when it is held in the branch vault, or when it is shipped between branches. Any further discussion here of these security procedures would be unwise, for obvious reasons, but they do make up a substantial proportion of a teller's working knowledge.

To facilitate counting, tellers try as much as possible to keep the money in straps. During lulls between customers, they count out one hundred bills of a single denomination to make up a strap. Should they begin to get too much money piled up at their work station, the teller must turn some of it over to the head teller for deposit in the branch vault. The head teller will only accept straps that have been counted and initialled by two separate tellers, so that preparation of money to be put into the vault necessarily becomes a cooperative venture among the tellers.

The training system. Basically, new tellers are trained by the same old-teach-new system that also prevailed in the Cone Department. The newly hired teller is assigned to watch one of the tellers work for a period of three or four days. During this time, the old teller is supposed to be explaining what she is doing as she goes through her work day. Toward the end of this training period, the new teller begins to carry on some of the transactions, while the old teller watches. When the head teller, who has been monitoring this process carefully, feels that the new teller is ready, she assigns the new teller "her" window. For the first few days, while the trainee operates her window, the training teller does not keep her window open but hovers behind the new teller, ready to help her out if a problem should arise. Eventually, the head teller decides that the trainee has grasped the basics well enough to operate her window on her own, and the training teller returns to her old work station.

Several of the current tellers were trained by the head teller. Everybody who went through that experience reports that it did not work out very well, because the head teller has so many other extraneous duties to perform that it is confusing to the new trainees, and because the head teller is so experienced and so quick that many of the procedures she follows are too habitualized for her to be able to explain them.

In addition to simply watching and listening, trainees are expected to take notes for future reference. Every trainee compiles a "training book," a bound ledger with a page devoted to each transaction or set of procedures that tellers must know how to do. In this ledger, the trainee tapes in sample copies of the various forms and documents

that must be filled out for each procedure, and
notes all the other formal and informal rules and
guidelines that must be followed. These training
books are not intended for permanent reference; it
is expected that after the first couple of months
all the information contained in them will have been
learned and assimilated by the teller. During these
first few months, the teller keeps the book nearby
at her window to consult when she runs into rare or
unusual customer requests that she has not yet
learned to carry out by heart.

It is necessary for all trainees to compile
their own training book because the bank has no
written record of these teller procedures. Although
the basic framework remains the same, these procedures are in a constant state of flux anyway. As
one of the tellers went over her one-year-old training book with me, it was necessary for her to point
out major or minor changes that have been made in
the operating procedures on every single page.

This method of carrying out the formal training
process is an effective method of passing on to the
trainees the hundreds of individual rules and guidelines that she must learn. The tellers reported,
however, that it took a period from a few weeks
to a couple of months after the training period before they were really able to figure out how all
these rules and guidelines fit together, what the
underlying logic was. In short, acquisition of the
banking paradigm did not occur until long after the
formal training program was complete. It is only
when they begin to pick up this paradigm, when they
have begun to intuitively recognize the principles
of double entry bookkeeping, and when they begin to
develop a feel for the types of customers and the
problems that they represent, it is only then that
they can put the training book aside and carry on as
fully functioning tellers without the aid of this
crutch. It takes even several more months before
the work becomes habitualized enough so that the
teller can carry it out without either intense
concentration or relatively frequent errors. New
tellers fail to settle up fairly regularly; old
experienced tellers hardly ever. It takes at least
six or eight months before the declining curve
begins to flatten out in the "hardly ever" region.
Further analysis of what is involved in this transition is presented later in this chapter.

Mr. Davis' lectures. Every month or two, the
branch manager gathers the employees together in the

81

conference room after the bank is closed to hear
some comments from Mr. Davis. Anthony Prezzi did
the same thing in the Cone Department, but while his
lectures were either ignored or ridiculed by the
workers, the comments that Mr. Davis makes are generally respected and remembered by the employees.
This is at least partially because the announcements
and pronouncements that Mr. Davis makes relate
directly to the tellers' jobs and result in changes
in the policies and procedures that they are supposed to follow. In the Cone Department, Prezzi tended to merely reiterate suggestions and exhortations
that had been ignored in the past and will be ignored again in the future.

    As the tellers remembered in their interviews,
Mr. Davis' recent lectures address themselves to
such topics as: the announcement of a Christmas
Club competition among the branches; announcement of
a change-over from the pass book to the statement
accounting system for savings accounts, with accomp-
anying suggestions for how to introduce this change
to the customers; new procedures developed by the
bank to follow in case members of any of the employees' families were kidnapped for the purpose of ex-
torting money from the bank; advice on what to do in
case of a robbery; and suggestions for how to better
simulate friendliness and courtesy in dealing with
the customers. With the possible exception of the
last topic, none of Mr. Davis' lectures fit into
the category of SOS (Same Old Shit), to borrow a
phrase from one of the Cone Department workers'
description of the lectures they heard from Prezzi.

    One of the main themes of these lectures is
the issue of security. Because the branch was robbed recently, and because of the element of threat
and danger involved, the employees are generally
vitally interested in what he has to say on this
subject. The other main theme that Mr. Davis tends
to dwell on is customer relations and how to improve them. The employees listen to the suggestions
he has to make on this subject with attitudes ranging from bemused tolerance to gratefulness. It
should be noted that Mr. Davis does not just exhort
people to be more friendly, but passes along specific suggestions for how to greet customers pleasant-
ly without slowing down the speed of the transaction.

Specific Working Knowledge

The tellers' working knowledge can be divided for the purposes of exposition into two distinct categories: the basic knowledge necessary to carry out the routine processing functions of the job; and the supplementary knowledge necessary to effectively handle the different types of problems that arise to interfere with this routine processing. The knowledge necessary to carry out the tellers' routine procedures is considerably more extensive and more varied than the knowledge routinely put to use by the machine operators in the Cone Department. Conversely, there seem to be fewer different types of problems that can potentially interfere with this routine work.

Knowledge about routine processing procedures. One of the most important routine processes that tellers must know how to do is to count money. This is one of those activities, like driving a car, that "everybody" knows how to do. But tellers, like professional drivers, learn how to do it both more carefully and more rapidly than everybody else. To count money accurately, the teller must touch each bill, feel it to make sure that two are not stuck together, and subconsciously count it. With the aid of "sticky finger", a commercial preparation applied to the hands to aid in the handling of money or other paper products, the best tellers can count money with complete accuracy at speeds that are too fast for the eye to follow. They learn to do it so almost-automatically that they can carry on conversations and do other kinds of work without either looking at the money they are counting or losing their count. In fact, tellers stated in their interviews that the most complete accuracy depends on doing the counting in this semi-automatic, habitualized way. It is only when they stop to think about what they are doing that they miscount or lose track of where they are. Similarly, in counting coins, tellers can count coins in groups of three, five, or even ten at a time, not noticing individual coins except as part of the pattern of the larger counting unit.

As an extension of the counting process, tellers learn to add and subtract "in their head" with more speed and facility than is normal among educated people in the society at large. Some tellers find this harder to do than others, and all tellers mention that in order to be a good teller one must be "good with figures". This ability does not require knowledge of any advanced mathematics beyond the grammar school level, but it does require that the teller feel comfortable and competent in the handling of simple mathematical calculations.

A second type of routine processing knowledge that tellers must have is the ability to operate a variety of office machinery. The most important of these is the adding machine. Each teller has her own adding machine at her own window, and it must be used on almost every transaction. It is primarily used for adding; subtraction occurs only with split deposits, or during the settling up process at the end of the day. For some transactions, the adding machine is used simply to record the amount of the transaction, even though no calculation is necessary. Unlike the clerks in some types of pre-computer office jobs, tellers do not use the adding machine frequently enough or consistently enough to really learn how to "touch add." In the Newton branch, the only touch adder is the head teller. In addition to the adding machine, certain procedures require the tellers to know how to operate a typewriter and two different kinds of check-writing machines that are located along the counter behind the tellers.

The third category of routine processing procedures that tellers need to know involves keeping up the running record of their activities. After each transaction, the money must be sorted, put away, and the money drawer closed. The documents used must be filed away in the money drawer (if they are "outs"), or in the works bin (if they are "ins"). The proper notation must be recorded on the "ins" pad, and memory-jogging details -- the customer's name or account number or the type of transaction -- must be written on to the adding machine tape next to the figures. Only after all these maintenance chores have been completed can the teller turn to the next customer or begin the next transaction.

The final and most widely inclusive category of routinely required working knowledge is the knowledge of all the different procedure sets that are required for each type of transaction. Each type of transaction has a set of procedures which covers

both the actions that the teller must undertake and
the rules and guidelines that she must follow as she
undertakes these actions. The most basic routine
function that makes up the teller's job is the
"operation" of their window. As the tellers operate
their windows the customers who come in may request
one or more services from among fifty different
possible transactions. Each transaction requested
is a separate alternative process. To replace tellers with "money machines" as several large national
banks have begun to do, the bank must require the
customer to standardize their requests and to choose
from a list of no more than eight or ten available
services. If the customers went to buy Travelers
Checks or use any service that is not on this short
list, they must come into the bank and deal with a
human teller. Given the present state of technology in the banking industry, the variety of services offered makes it necessary for banks to have
human tellers processing their customers' requests,
basically without the aid of any machine more complex than the teller's adding machine.

A very important part of the tellers' job is
the quality control function: the counting, adding,
and record-keeping functions that the tellers perform. According to the tellers interviewed, high
quality work in their job means accurate work. By
analogy, then, quality control would refer to the
verification of accuracy that is such an important
part of the teller's job. One of the tellers even
put it this way: "That's what we're basically here
for, to count money."

Supplementary working knowledge. The principal
pressure on tellers from the management is to maintain complete accuracy, to avoid shortages and overages in the daily settlements. Weekly and monthly
records are kept on each teller's overages or shortages. It is these records that form the principal
basis for management's quarterly evaluations of the
tellers. If tellers should desire to get a job as
a teller with another bank in the future, that bank
will call the Arnold Bank to check out these settlement records. In response to this pressure, tellers
develop a variety of techniques and strategies which
they find help them to avoid errors.

First of all, to avoid simple mistakes, tellers
feel that it is not enough simply to know the rules
and procedures. Before the teller can get in the
groove of doing the right thing naturally, without
thinking specifically about each detail, she must

85

get an understanding of the reasons why things are done the way that they are.

> Ins and outs -- none of it made any sense to me at all .... It took me quite a long time to catch on. It's relatively simple once you get the idea and concept behind the jobs. (Q: "What do you mean, idea and concept?") How everything goes in its place and fits together. You've got to understand why you do things, which you can't see until you get the overall view of what you're doing and how everything has to balance out each other in the credit and debits sides. Everything you do to one side, you have to do something to the other side to make it equal. You've just got to know the general pattern -- how it all fits together. Once you get that in your head, then you can see why you have to put something in the drawer and some in works and where everything belongs.

Once this paradigm has been acquired, which usually takes a couple of months after starting work,

> Everybody has their own system. You trial and error different ways in the beginning until you find what works best for you.

Although certain rules and procedures are required by the bank for each type of transaction, each teller develops her own way of handling the transaction as a whole, of combining these different required elements into her own unique system. Yet the transactions are still basically similar enough so that it is possible for tellers to "read" each other's adding machine tape, if necessary, when they help each other to search out the causes of settlement errors.

Each of these individual transaction-processing systems combines the required elements set down by the bank with certain additional elements that each teller uses to help herself recall the customer and the transaction, should that become necessary. Usually these additional elements involve a system of code notations on the adding machine tape, but some tellers also record different information on the "ins" pad, too.

86

Whatever the system the teller chooses to
follow, to avoid errors she must learn to follow it
as a matter of unthinking habit. Tellers strongly
emphasized the necessity of developing strong habits
and relying on them to carry one through day after
day. Without these habits, it would be impossible
to carry on virutally error-free work for such long
periods of time. (The present record at the Newton
branch is six months without a settlement error.)

> Its got to be on a sub-conscious level
> really. Your pattern is so fully devel-
> oped and on such an instinct basis you
> can talk to customers and still do it
> right.

Yet, curiously, as tellers develop their ability to
carry out these transactions habitually, they simultaneously develop their powers of recall. Even
though they are no longer concentrating so much conscious attention on each transaction, as they gain
more experience they find it progressively easier to
remember more specific details of each transaction
from reading the adding machine tape.

> I've been so busy, I don't know what's
> going on, but when you look back on the
> tape you remember.

One teller even reported that as she got more experienced, she began not to worry about recording
so much data on the adding machine tape, since she
could remember the customers and their transactions
from the numbers alone.
   Using these error-avoidance strategies and taking such elementary precautions as double and triple
counting everything, experienced tellers are able to
maintain a remarkable record of error-free work.
The typical experienced teller manages to go a
month or two between settlement failures -- an
average of only seven or eight mistakes a year.
Tellers don't feel especially proud of this, since
the normative performance standard in their occupa-
tion is zero errors per year, nevertheless it is a
remarkable rate compared with the defect rates that
quality control departments in other industries and
occupations accept as normal.
   Another type of "mistake" that happens much
less frequently, but which tellers are nevertheless
just as anxious to avoid, is the acceptance of a
bad check or some other form of customer transaction

that causes the bank to lose money. Even though this is a relatively rare occurrence, it happens every once in a whole to every teller, and whenever it does, the bank makes a special point of letting the individual teller know about it. To avoid being taken by such "bad eggs" (as Mr. Davis calls them), the tellers have developed a repertoire of signs and hints that they take as indicators that the transaction that a particular customer proposes might be a troublesome one. On the most obvious level, tellers remember the names of customers who have had checks bounce frequently in the past, and warn each other about them. But they have also developed more subtle ways of predicting possible trouble. Tellers mistrust people who change their minds suddenly while in the midst of a transaction at the window, or who in other ways seem to be trying to get the tellers confused. They know the street addresses of the subsidized housing projects in the Newton area, and they are more careful with customers from those addresses, not necessarily because they mistrust them more, but because "people are poorer over there, and so they have more money problems."* They are suspicious about people who are trying to cash checks that according to the trial balance will virtually close the account, but who don't ask to have the account closed. Checks that are "stale", i.e., dated long ago, also arouse suspicion.

If for any reason a teller is uneasy about a particular customer or transaction, there are several steps she can take. She can ask for an ID, or ask the customer to sign the check again on the back, to obtain another signature for comparison purposes. She can log the check in on the DAD machine, a device which marks the check with the precise date and time that it was cashed, and which also triggers the bank's camera to take a picture of the customers. Finally, she can require the customer to get the signature of a bank officer before she will carry out the transaction. According to bank policy, there are many conditions under which she must do this anyway -- postdated checks, checks over $400, etc. -- but it is at the teller's discretion to send somebody to a bank officer if for any reason she has doubts.

---

*A teller who lives in one of these projects herself reported this statement made to her by the teller who was training her when she first went to work at the bank.

At the teller windows inside the building, where it is possible for tellers to see their customers coming and look them over before they actually step up to her window and request her services, tellers develop ways of sizing up and categorizing customers who are potentially "good" as well as bad. At least in the tellers' opinions, mere possession of a lot of money in their accounts is not sufficient to qualify people as "good" customers, although it helps. The most important attribute of good customers seems to be that they use the bank's services regularly. They come in often, and they get to know the tellers personally. The "best" customers in this respect are the thirty or forty businesses and offices in the Newton shopping center. Tellers estimate that they spend fifty percent of their time servicing these thirty or forty business accounts. In addition to these business accounts, there are other individuals who enjoy the status of good customers because they maintain active savings and checking accounts and come in often. Also counted as good customers are people who are as pleasant and friendly to the tellers as the tellers are to them, or older customers, identifiable by their low account numbers, who have been with the branch since it opened.

Although full time tellers get to know most of the customers at least well enough to recognize their faces, good customers get some special treatment beyond that which is accorded to customers who are only known and recognized. Known customers can get their checks processed faster because the teller does not have to look up their signatures in the file cards. For good customers, the teller does not bother to look up the trial balance either, thus eliminating both of these time-consuming procedures. Good customers are also generally treated with a little extra courtesy. For instance, if a bank officer's signature is necessary, the teller will go back and get it herself. In other cases, she will send the customers back themselves. This keeps the line moving and is therefore more efficient, but it requires the customers to wait in line again once they have gotten the proper signature.*

---

*Though pleasant people are "good customers," unpleasant customers are not necessarily put into the "bad customer" category. Bad customers are people who are potential problems for the bank as an institution, not for its tellers, who accept them as part of the job.

A very general type of customer typology is apparently employed by the full time tellers. There are good customers, known customers, bad customers, and the residual category of unknown customers. Actually, there is also a very small fifth category of celebrity customers, people whose identity is known to the tellers even before they step into the bank for the first time. At the Newton branch, this category consists of a few of the pro-football players from the central city's NFL team, who have apartments in the Newton area. The tellers find it interesting to be in the position of having personal knowledge of the financial doings of these athletes with their legendary high salaries.

Although these typologies of individual customers are somewhat helpful in predicting the situations that the teller is going to encounter, knowledge about collective patterns of customer behavior is more significant, and more carefully observed. The bank's business has predictable rhythms of customer activity, rhythms that run in daily, weekly, and bi-weekly cycles. Each day, the rate of customer traffic builds up slowly through the morning, picking up more rapidly after eleven, heading for the daily peak at the lunch hour, tapering off slowly in the afternoon, then picking up again slightly in the last few minutes before closing. Knowledge of this daily cycle allows tellers to predict when they are going to have time to count down money, put up straps, process the mail, and buy or sell each other the specialized transactions. There is also a strong weekly pattern, with the heaviest crush of customers coming on Friday, Friday night and Saturday, which is the period immediately after most customers receive their pay checks. Monday is also a busy day because the weekend is the peak time for their business customers, who fill the night depository with work all weekend, and who come in on Monday with even more transactions to be effected. Tuesdays and Wednesdays are the slowest days. A few people get paid and shop on Thursdays, so it is somewhat busier than the two days before it.

Most of the Newton branch's customers are white collar workers, who are generally paid monthly or bi-weekly. This contributes monthly and bi-weekly cycles that overlie the weekly and daily ones. End-of-month Fridays are the busiest days that there are at the bank. Cashing checks non-stop all day, a teller at a drive-in window can have as much as $30,000 worth of "outs" on such a day. During such a day, the bank is crowded from opening to close;

90

there are lines at every window; and the tellers
work like demons all day to try to keep up. Fridays
that come at the middle of the month are also
noticeably busier than other Fridays, because some
people are paid bi-weekly and because some of the
largest employers in the area divide their monthly
payroll, paying half of the work force every two
weeks. Tellers know when such periods of peak
activity are coming up, and they prepare for them by
"buying" extra money from the vault.

In addition to this customer-predicting knowledge, tellers also develop techniques for handling
the customers and keeping them happy. They do this
both because "customer relations" is an important
part of their job, one that is stressed by Mr. Davis,
and also because these techniques help them to
"handle" their customers to some extent by setting
the terms of the interaction. All of these techniques require a certain basic level of proficiency
in the routine processing of the transaction that
the customers bring to the window. Until that level
of proficiency is reached, many of these customer
relations techniques are not possible. The techniques, as listed by one of the tellers whom the other
tellers felt was pretty good at this aspect of her
job, include the following: looking customers in
the eye and maintaining the eye contact; greeting
them directly ("Hello, how are you today?"); saying
something pleasant or complimentary about their
apparent mood ("You look happy today.") or their
clothes or their kids or the weather or the time or
whatever, but never about the transaction itself;*
when the transaction is complete, saying good-bye to
the customer personally, using the name furnished by
the customer on the check or deposit slip ("Good-
bye, Mr. Smith, have a happy day."). All of these
customer-pleasing techniques require that the teller

---

*In this exchange of pleasantries, the teller gives the
appearance of temporarily stepping out of her role as
teller and striking up a friendly personal conversation.
Since the financial business being transacted is generally considered to be a very personal and confidential
part of their customer's life, it is not appropriate for
the teller to comment on it or even to appear to notice
it while chatting with a customer in this pseudo-
personal manner. This is a delicate problem. The customer's transactions must be discussed only in the most
business-like and impersonal manner, yet each customer
should be also addressed in a friendly and personal mood.

be able to go through the motions of handling the transaction automatically, while talking and maintaining eye contact with the customer on a completely separate subject. Yet through all this, speed and accuracy must be maintained.

> Do it with speed, but be friendly at
> the same time, that's what you've got
> to do. Friendly but slow, the cus-
> tomers aren't going to be happy if
> they have to stand in line.

The techniques for handling angry or irritated customers are just the opposite. Customers who are upset are not interested in friendliness, they want business-like efficiency. The tellers respond by verbally distancing themselves from the interaction. They try to efface their own personality and become simply representatives of the bank. All the tellers felt that in this situation the most important thing to do is to keep one's cool and not lose one's temper. They inform the customer of the relevant bank policies that caused whatever action of the bank it was that got the customer upset. "If a customer is completely irrational," or if it otherwise appears that the customer is really more interested in "telling off" the bank than he is in having the teller perform some specific service, then the teller tries to send the customer to Mr. Davis or his assistant.

> The main thing is, you can't let them
> get mad at you. It's the bank they're
> mad at. Let them go talk to somebody
> who's in charge of the bank. Usually
> it's something I'm not authorized to
> do anything about anyway.

The teller's basic strategy for handling this kind of customer, therefore, involves two steps. First, the teller becomes very business-like and impersonal herself. If this does not cause the customer to calm down and become more business-like also, then the teller passes the customer along to management.

During peak business periods, when the lines are long and most of the customers are at least a little grumpy by the time they arrive at the window, then it is especially important that the teller seize the initiative in the interaction.

> Find something about them and make a
> friendly comment, a little compliment,
> right when they first come up with their
> check or whatever.

This sets a tone that makes it hard for the customer
to harrass the teller about the long wait, an unpleasant experience for the teller, and a time-
consuming one, too, that merely lengthens the wait
of the other customers in line.

All of these supplementary techniques which
tellers use to collectively manage the money, manage the paper-work, manage the customers, through
the business day -- all this know-how contributes
to the success of the branch and of the Arnold
National Bank, but it also contributes to the tellers' own well-being, too. One part time teller
summed up her interview so well, let her statement
sum up this chapter too:

> There's the constant pressure, and
> sometimes it's so monotonous, and try-
> ing to be nice to customers even if
> they're not nice to you. But lately,
> with everything going so smooth and
> everybody doing such a good job, some-
> times it makes you feel good just being
> a part of it, even if it is just a
> crummy part time job.

4. Other Workplaces

Collected here are capsule descriptions of
other work situations that were studied in the
course of the research. Originally, these interviews were conducted either as part of the pre-testing of the interview schedule or as an attempt to
undertake a full case study. Although the interviews were not originally conducted for this purpose, the data collected about these work situations
provided valuable comparative perspective for the
material collected in the case studies. Since the
generalizations made in Part II of this work are
often grounded in the data collected about these
other work situations as well as the two full-scale
case studies, these descriptions are necessary to
introduce the work situations to the reader.
   The descriptions of the work situations presented here are based in each case on interviews
with only one person in the work situation.* The
material presented in this chapter is thus of less
certain validity than the case studies, where it
was possible to check each piece of information
with at least two informants. The second limitation
of this material derives from the mode of presentation. In order to present these ten work situations, the description of each case must be kept so
short that much interesting and even theoretically
relevant detail has to be left out. Nevertheless,
this survey over a range of blue collar and white
collar jobs is an important part of the research.
It provides the comparative context necessary to
interpret specific elements of the work situations
discussed in detail in the case studies, and to per-

---

*Except for the meat cutters, two of whom were interviewed.

mit a range of theoretical generalization that would not be possible based on the two case studies alone.

The Warehouse Worker

This man works in the main warehouse of a family-owned hardware wholesaling firm. The company has expanded over the last few years, opening two branch warehouses in neighboring states. It serves two different types of customers, hardware stores and construction contractors.

At one time the owner, his secretary, and the salesmen worked out of the front office attached to the main warehouse, but at the time of the expansion the headquarters of the company's operations were moved into separate offices in another building several blocks away. The front office is now occupied only by the warehouse manager and his secretary. The rest of the warehouse staff consists of eight full-time "chasers," three truck drivers, and from one to five part-time chasers, depending on the season. Chasers have two principal tasks: "stocking up" the goods as they are delivered from the manufacturers, verifying the shipments, checking for hidden damage, and sorting out the different items into their proper places in the racks; and "chasing down" the various items that customers have ordered, collecting the different items that make up the order and bringing them together at the loading dock.

The warehouse itself is divided into three sections, depending on the type of "rack", or storage facility, that each section contains. Small parts are located in bins along two walls of the warehouse. Most of the stock is kept on regular shelves that take up the central area of the warehouse. There is a separate area at the rear with wide aisles and much larger shelves, where large items are stored on skids, just as they come off the trucks. One of the chasers operates the fork lift truck and is informally in charge of this rear section. Except for him, all of the other chasers do the same type of work and there is no division of labor among them.

The working knowledge that the chasers must have primarily involves knowing the location of the thousands of different items stocked. There are catalogs that contain this information, but nobody consults them. New chasers find things by asking older chasers where they are. The stock is constantly shifting, as new items are added and old items are closed out, so that once an experienced chaser has learned where everything is, he must keep up with it, as there are constant small changes being made.

The crew of chasers is made up of two distinct groups. There are three older white men who have been with the company for many years, and who know the owner relatively well since he worked right there in the warehouse up until a few years ago. The warehouse manager is a former member of this group of chasers, as he had previously been for many years the working foreman of the chasers. He moved up to the newly created job of warehouse manager when the rest of the management was moved out. The rest of the chasers, including my informant, had all worked there less than five years. Except for one Puerto Rican, they are all black. They are much less committed to the company or the job, and they have no personal relationship with the owner. The part-time chasers are hired on a temporary basis. They are usually high school or college students, and they are almost always white.

In addition to the changing composition of the work force of the chasers, two other significant changes have recently affected the work. When the two branch warehouses were opened up, the company introduced a computerized inventory control system. Previously, the chasers were putting together the customers' orders from a copy of the hand-written sales slip. Now the orders come to the warehouse by data transmission telephone line from the computer in the central office to a computer printout station in the warehouse. These computerized orders contain not only the name and numbers of the items required but also the ostensible location of each item in the warehouse. (To prepare for this computerization, each bin and shelf in the warehouse was numbered.)

This would have the effect of totally eliminating the necessity for the chasers' main body of working knowledge, knowledge of the location of parts. So far, however, the computer has not performed as expected, since a relatively large proportion of the items in the warehouse are not located in the place where the computer's memory bank says that they are. This is because the computer was programmed based on the parts catalog which had supposedly served as the guide for the chasers, but since the chasers never actually used that catalog, they never kept it up to date. Therefore, the original locations for many of the items were programmed into the computer incorrectly, and there is

97

no systematic provision for discovering and cor-
recting these errors. As a result, the chasers more
or less ignore the location instructions on the computer printouts that they are working from, just as
they had ignored the catalog in the past. It is in
their interest, of course, to try and perpetuate the
informal system whereby they are the only people in
the company who know exactly where any particular
item is located. They do not do this consciously,
but they do consciously enjoy the implicit competition with the computer, in which the computer is so
often wrong and they are so often right.

The computer has had the effect of tightening
up the inventory control system. Before the computer was installed, it was possible for the chasers
to take home any small inexpensive items that they
needed for their own use around the house. As long
as nobody became greedy, this was considered a
pleasant fringe benefit of their job, and there was
no indication that the inventory losses were large
enough to provoke management into taking any kind of
action. The computerized inventory control system,
however, now keeps an exact record of the numbers
of any particular item on hand. This has made it
possible to cut total inventory by re-ordering items
only when their numbers get quite low. Under these
conditions, the pilferage that occurs is much more
likely to come to management's attention, and workers now feel that it is only safe to take very small
items -- like nails or screws -- that are invento-
ried by weight instead of by number.

Another recent change that has had repercus-
sions for the chasers is the unionization of the
truck drivers. In the past, there had been recurrent difficulties when the company's non-union
drivers attempted to make deliveries to unionized
construction sites. Recently, the management and
the Teamsters Union agreed to have the truck drivers
join the union in order to avoid these problems.
The truck drivers, although they are happy with the
move, were not "organized" in any conventional sense
of the word, and were in fact notified of their im-
pending unionization by management. Since the
chasers have also been wanting to join the union,
but two of the older white chasers have strong anti-
union feelings and are opposed to the idea. At the
time of the interview, the young chasers were still
talking union, but they had never met a union representative, had no idea how to get in touch with one,
and were basically just waiting and hoping that the
Teamsters would come to them.

The Truck Driver

This man and twenty other truckers work for the
Internal Transport Department in a main plant of
one of the largest corporations in the United States. Their department is located in one of the
smaller buildings in a large diversified plant, made
up of almost a hundred separate buildings covering
several square miles and employing over twenty
thousand people.

The Internal Transport Department has three
related functions: it receives goods from outside
suppliers at its loading docks and distributes them
among the various buildings in the plant; it transports materials from one building to another within
the plant; and it transports goods between this
plant and the twenty other plants of the same corporation that are located within a two hundred mile
radius.

The personnel of the Internal Transport Department consists of the twenty truckers, a five-man
loading crew, three management personnel, and a
four-woman office staff. The truckers and the loading crew are all members of the Teamsters Union.
Although the loading crew does not actually drive
trucks, all have the necessary drivers' permits and
are serving a sort of apprenticeship that lasts up
to two years before they acquire enough seniority
to be assigned a truck.

Almost all of the work in the department is
organized into a routine of regularly scheduled
daily runs with a particular schedule of pickups
and deliveries. About half of these runs remain
entirely within the confines of the plant, shuttling
back and forth among the buildings. The other
regularly scheduled runs cover several of the plants
in the area. These runs are assigned completely on
the basis of seniority, with the most senior worker
getting first choice and so on down the line. The
outside runs are the most desirable, because there
is more unsupervised driving time between stops, and
the driver therefore has more opportunity to hustle
through part of the run in order to make extra time
to stop off for lunch somewhere or to drop in on
friends. A few of the daily runs take ten or eleven
hours to complete, and the workers who have chosen
these runs are therefore guaranteed ten or fifteen
hours of overtime every week.

Except that all pickups and deliveries are made
among the different locations of the same corpora-

99

tion, work in the Internal Transport Department is
similar to work in trucking terminals anywhere else
in the trucking industry. After arriving at work in
the morning, each trucker picks up the tickets
describing the stops that are to be made on the run
and the cargo that is to be picked up or delivered
at each stop. Working along with the loading crew,
he then supervises the loading of any material on
the dock that is to be delivered during his run.
Truck loading is a complex operation involving a
great deal of working knowledge. Careful calculations of weight must be made, since the weight distribution of the load is a crucial safety factor,
and each item must be packed in in such a way so
that it will not shift or fall during the run. This
is necessary both to maintain safety and to prevent
damage to the goods. Once the truck is properly
loaded, the driver leaves on his run. At some of
the stops he must load and unload the material himself; at other stops there are loading crews whose
union contracts prohibit the drivers from helping
out, and the driver can take a break while the truck
is being loaded.

Because of the way the seniority system operates to periodically allow men to choose better rou-
tes, because of the relatively high pay, and because
of the relative freedom from close supervision in
comparison with other jobs in the plant, the truckers are quite satisfied with their work. This high
job satisfaction, however, does not lead to feelings
of commitment to the corporation. Negotiations over
the last few contracts have led to bitter strikes,
one of them lasting several months. On all these
occasions, the workers in this plant have been forced back to work because a majority of the workers
nationally have accepted the new contract, even
though the workers in this plant have turned out
large majorities in favor of holding out for a
better contract.

The Welder

This man works in the Weld and Solder Department of a plant that manufactures truck radiators.
There are about forty workers in this department,
about three hundred in the whole plant. The plant
is located in the inner city, in a neighborhood
which was once predominantly Italian but which is
now entirely black. Most of the workers with twenty
or more years seniority (about one-third of the work

force) are Italians; almost all of the younger workers are black.

The company was founded about forty years ago
by an Italian family, who sold out in the late '60's
to an auto parts conglomerate. After two years of
an unsuccessful attempt to transform and expand the
company's operations, an attempt which led to intense conflict between the workers and the new managers, the company was again sold, this time to an
even larger conglomerate. The new owners have re-
turned the plant to a mode of operation that is more
similar to the former operation under the original
owners. Through all these changes, the workforce
has been represented by a local of the United Auto
Workers union, which has been the bargaining agent
since the late 1940's.

The Weld and Solder Department is responsible
for the last assembly operation in the manufacture
of radiators. The radiator cores are manufactured
upstairs on the second floor of the plant; the
frames are manufactured downstairs. After the frame
parts have been cut out in the Sheet Metal Department and pressed into shape in the Stamping Department, the Weld and Solder Department is responsible
for welding the frames together and soldering the
cores into the frames. After this operation, the
only other functions still remaining are those of
the Quality Control Department and the Packing Department.

Although there is some automated material
handling equipment, especially upstairs in the Core
Department, this is not an assembly line operation.
The materials to be welded are brought to each
worker's station on specially built pallets carried
by forklift trucks. As the welder finishes each
piece, he stacks it on another pallet to be eventually moved on to the next operation. The plant
specializes in the small batch production of various
specialized types of heavy duty radiators. Each
customer's order involves variation in the shape of
the frame, the construction techniques, and the type
of metal used. There are also different types of
cores, as well as different sizes. For this reason
there is little specialization in the Weld and Solder Department. Although all the workers in the
department are called welders, they actually spend
more than half their time soldering. Since there is
so much variation in the materials used, each worker
must master a wide variety of specific soldering
and welding techniques.

All the welders in the department are paid
according to an individual piece work incentive
system. As each new batch of radiators comes into
the department, the work is scheduled so that one
worker is responsible for all of the welds or sol-
ders of a particular type called for by the specifications of that particular batch. Normally, each
particular weld or solder has already been timed
out, so that the industrial engineers merely add up
the times of the different operations assigned to a
particular worker to compute the rate for each job.
The average batch or "run" only spends two or three
days in the department, so the workers are normally
assigned new jobs and new rates every day or two,
or even several times in the same day on short runs.
Because of these short runs, and the variation
between the different orders, it has not been possible to introduce much routinization or detailed
specialization within the department. Each welder
is expected to learn all the different techniques
that might be necessary, and each welder experiences
a relatively high amount of variation as his task is
switched from one batch to the next.
The most difficult problem that these workers
have to deal with stems from the fact that the
copper in the radiator cores is soft and will melt
at lower temperatures than the metals in the frame.
For this reason, any welding that must be done to
the frame after the core has already been inserted
is a delicate operation. These operations are
generally assigned to the older, experienced workers. The basic technique involves accomplishing the
weld as rapidly as possible using the absolute
minimum amount of heat necessary to successfully
complete the weld.
Because of the lack of routinization and
because of the piece work pay scale, welders acquire
a very large body of working knowledge, since they
need to know not only each different welding or
soldering technique, but also an array of short cuts
for each technique that will allow them to "make
out" a decent average hourly wage without working
excessively hard.*

The Meatcutters

The two men interviewed are both meat cutters
in different branches of the same chain of super-

_____

*A very similar work situation is described by Roy (1955).

markets. Both are members of the Meatcutters Union.
One has practiced this trade since he learned it in
the Army eight years ago, the other has learned it
over the course of the two years which he had been
employed, first part-time and then full-time, by
this company. The more experienced worker is the
head of the meat department at his store, a working
foreman's job that carries the title of "Meat Head."
The second worker is the "head" of the one-man fresh
fish department in his store, a position known as
"Fish Head."*

Supermarket meatcutters are considered to be
skilled workers, practitioners of the butcher's
trade, which has had a long and honorable history
as an independent craft. The main body of working
knowledge in this craft consists of three elements:
knowledge of the anatomy of a variety of animals;
knowledge of certain standardized ways of dividing
the carcass into the cuts of meat sanctioned by
tradition and consumer preference; and knowledge of
safe and sanitary work procedures.

The older meatcutter was given at least a token
overall training in this traditional trade by the
short intensive course given to him in the Army.
The younger man was hired without any prior experience to work in the fish department and has learned
on the job how to butcher fish, but not any other
types of meat. Although he has acquired the pay,
status, and occupational title of meatcutter because
of the formal requirements of the union contract,
he is basically a retail clerk who has learned how
to clean and cut fish, as other retail clerks have
learned how to package produce or operate cash
registers.

These differences in training reflect profound
changes in the meatcutters' trade as a result of new
innovations in the organization of work that are
being introduced throughout the industry. Three
years ago this chain stopped butchering sides of
beef, lamb or pork in the retail stores. Two years
ago it stopped butchering poultry. The chain now
has one central meat cutting plant where the actual
butchering takes place, organized on the same kind
of rationalized assembly-line principles that were

---

*These colorful job titles are common in the industry, and
common usage has erased any trace of humor. The other
position of responsibility among the meatcutters is that of
the "Deli Head."

already introduced into the meat packing industry in the late nineteenth century.

The retail stores now receive their meat from that plant already cut up into large retail cuts and packed in refrigerated containers. At the store, the meatcutters open the containers, cut some of the larger portions into smaller units, put the meat on a plastic tray and feed it into the machine that wraps, weighs, and labels each item. Even hamburger is already preground; it is reground again in the stores only to make it look better. Under this new organization of work, the number of meatcutters in the retail stores has been reduced by half. The main function of those remaining is to operate the wrapping machine and to stock the cases. Meatcutters still perform special customer requests, but there are many fewer of these since the stores have adopted new physical layouts which place the butchers out of sight behind one-way glass.

Poultry now arrives from the processors already cut up, packed, labeled, and "chilled" or semi-frozen. The only thing the meatcutters have to do with it is to keep the cases stocked. Almost all the branches of the chain have phased out their fresh fish departments, replacing them with expanded frozen fish sections. The frozen fish is also prepacked, and the meatcutter's only job is to stock it. A few large stores in ethnic neighborhoods where customers have traditionally bought a high volume of fresh fish still retain these departments.

The "fish head" interviewed works in one such store. Wednesday afternoon through Saturday morning he operates the fresh fish department. Mondays he has off, and Tuesdays he mainly takes inventory and checks and cleans the frozen fish case. Because of this arrangement the job is relatively autonomous. Because he is in the Meatcutters Union, the pay is relatively good. Nevertheless, he is not very satisfied with his work. He does not identify himself with the meatcutting trade, and he thinks being a fish cutter is too low status a job for a community college graduate. In any case, there is no future in the trade -- he expects that the chain will eventually close the fresh fish department even in his store, although it does the highest volume of business in the chain.

The meat head also realizes he is in a dying trade, but he has aspirations to move eventually into management. He now spends most of his time keeping inventory and scheduling the workers in his

department. He would like to see the Meat Head's
job separated from the union and made a formal part
of management, with the same kind of incentive bonus
based on volume that is part of the pay system of
other managerial personnel.

The older meatcutters in the department complain bitterly about the change in their job, feeling that they have been reduced to nothing more than
"glorified retail clerks." When they voice this
complaint at union meetings, however, the union
representatives take the position that it was a
great union victory to retain their jobs at all,
since the company wanted originally to run the meat
department entirely with lower paid retail clerks,
using former meatcutters only as department managers.

The Longshoreman

The longshoreman interviewed works the docks of
a large East Coat port, a job he has held for the
past three years. This is a diversified port,
offering a variety of specialized docking facilities
for the handling of different types of cargo: new
containerized facilities; traditional break-bulk
docks, fuel depots for oil, port side grain elevators, and specialized facilities for the unloading
and storage of automobiles, coal, and sand and
gravel.

The port is completely unionized, and all work
on the docks is assigned through the union's hiring
hall. By union contract, any transfer of material
between ship and shore must be carried out by longshoremen, even in the case of the oil depot where
the only work involved is the connection of a few
hoses and the opening of a few valves, followed by a
wait of several hours until the time has come to
close the valves and disconnect.

Longshore work is organized into work gangs
each with its own leader or gang boss. Accordingly,
there are two strata of longshoremen, a higher
strata of permanent gang members and a lower strata
of extra men called in when a gang needs to be
temporarily enlarged for a particular work assignment. The man interviewed had just been made a
regular member of a gang after almost three years of
work in the port. This is an important step, one
that he expected would result in more work, increased earnings, and much improved working conditions.

105

When the union receives a request for long-shoremen from one of the companies in port, it calls a gang boss and assigns him to the job. Automatically the other three men in his gang (Four men is the normal gang size, although a few gangs have as many as eight or ten.) are assigned to the job also, meaning that regular gang members get their work assignments without having to waste hours hanging around the hiring hall. If the job calls for more men than the gang has members, then the extra men are chosen by the union from among the people in the hiring hall and sent out to join the gang on the work site. This system means that gang members are assured of more regular work assignments and a steadier rate of pay, as well as the opportunity to work regularly with the same group of people. There is no formal procedure for appointing longshoremen to work gangs. When a gang boss has a vacancy, he appoints a friend or somebody that the gang has gotten along well with when they have worked together in the past.

In a diversified port like this one, longshore-men encounter a wide variety of work materials, technologies, and environments as they move from assignment to assignment. This variation in the work requires the longshoremen to pick up a large stock of working knowledge. Each different material or technological arrangement requires a different set of work practices, a different means of physical transport (crane, pump, vacuum system, or other), a different technique for "hooking up" the cargo to the transport mechanism, a different set of stand-ardized systems for the division of work tasks with-in the gang, and a different set of safety precautions.

In the traditional break-bulk system each item in the cargo is individually moved from the dock to a cargo net and from the net to a particular place in the ship's hold, where it must be packed care-fully in with the rest of the cargo, to prevent the cargo from breaking up and shifting around at sea. This traditional technology is still used by some small freight lines and even by large companies on modern ships, when the cargo involved is moving to or from smaller ports in the less developed parts of the world. A whole occupational culture has built up around this traditional technique, with its own jargon, its own prescribed pattern of work gang interaction, and its own techniques to ensure the safety of members of the gang under these dangerous work conditions.

106

In a more modern system small individual items
of cargo are now more normally handled on skids.
Often the whole load on the skid has been "shrink
wrapped," a process that attaches the cargo to a
skid by encasing the whole package in a tough coat
of waterproof plastic. A different set of techniques is necessary to handle cargo on skids, along
with a different set of safety precautions.

Over in the containerized section of the port,
an even more capital intensive new technology allows
more tons of the same type of cargo to be handled
more quickly by fewer longshoremen. Once again,
this new technology has fostered the development of
another array of techniques for parceling out the
work tasks within the gang, hooking up the containers, and keeping safe.

Likewise, special types of cargo that are
handled by the port in large quantities are provided
with specialized facilities. Ramp-loading automobiles, chute-loading gravel -- each has its own
specialized work procedures requiring the development of still more specialized knowledge.

After three years in the port, the longshoreman
feels he was still learning "something new every
day." The high pay, the chance to work regularly
with friends on his gang, and the variety between
work assignments -- all contribute to his feeling
that he has landed a good job.

The Production Control Clerk

This woman works in the district office of a
government agency that is responsible for making
major repairs on buildings owned or leased by the
government. Twenty-six employees in her district
are responsible for nine office buildings. Each of
these buildings has its own staff of maintenance
workers who perform routine maintenance. Major repairs and renovations classified as capital expenditures are carried out by private contractors, whose
work is overseen by a different agency. The department in which this woman works is made up primarily
of electricians, plumbers and other craftsmen. They
handle all repair jobs that are neither small enough
to be classifed as routine maintenance nor large
enough to be considered capital expenditures.

The department personnel consists of an office
staff of six people and a twenty-person maintenance
staff, made up of skilled craftsmen representing
most of the building trades -- electricians, plumb-

ers, carpenters, painters, etc. Two of these men
are general foremen, and four others are working
foremen, each in charge of one of the trades that
includes two or more workers. Some of the crafts
are represented in the department by only one worker, like the elevator man and the plasterer. The
maintenance staff is all male, all black, and mostly
over forty years old. /Generally, these are men who
had somehow learned their trade in an era when the
various construction unions were closed to blacks,
so they were forced to turn to these lower paying
government jobs. Over the last decade, however,
these men have been represented by a union of blue
collar government workers. Under recent standards
of comparability with private industry, their pay
has steadily improved and is presently comparable
with that of construction workers outside the
government. Being government work, the security and
fringe benefits are much better than work in the
construction industry generally. These benefits
combined with the higher pay scales mean that these
men's jobs, at least in their own opinion are now
much better than normal construction work outside.

The office staff consists of a department manager and an assistant manager, both white males.
They have an administrative assistant, an older
white woman who is the immediate superior for the
other three women who work in the office. Two pay
grades below the administrative assistant is the
production control clerk, and two pay grades below
her are a typist and a woman who is nominally a file
clerk, but who also types and answers the telephone.
The hierarchy within the office is manifested in its
physical layout. The desk of the file clerk is
located right inside the door to the office. Strung
out behind her in ascending order are the desk of
the typist; an empty desk used by the foremen when
they are in; the production clerk's desk; the administrative assistant's work area; the assistant manager's work area, set off from the rest of the
office by a make-shift arrangement of file cabinets;
and finally the manager's office, which is actually
a separate room with its own access door out into
the hall of the building.

There is no camaraderie among the office staff
at all, little if any informal interaction. At
lunch time and break times, all of the workers leave
the office and go their separate ways. Age, race
and class distinctions separate each of the women
from the others. The administrative assistant and
the typist are both older white women who have work-

108

ed in the department for years, but they have little to say to each other. As the production clerk sees it, the typist is a "low class person" from a southern rural background, and the administrative assistant is "very middle class," courteously formal in her relations with the lower status women in the office. The file clerk job has in recent years been filled by a succession of young black or Spanish women fresh out of high school.

The production control clerk is a black woman in her mid-thirties. Starting work for the government ten years ago in the lowest possible white collar pay grade, she has worked her way up through a succession of jobs to her present position, which she has held for the past three years. She has taken advantage of a number of programs that the government sponsors to upgrade the job skills of its minority employees, to the point where she is now "over qualified" for her production clerk's position. She hopes soon to be able to move up to an administrative assistant's position if one opens up in another district, but this will be difficult. For the first time in her government career, she is getting mediocre job ratings in the bi-annual evaluations. The administrative assistant is responsible for making these ratings and she always routinely gives mediocre ratings to her subordinates.

The task of the production control clerk is to keep a record of all expenditures on each repair job undertaken by the department. These expenditures include both materials requisitioned and the hours that the maintenance staff puts in. To accomplish a repair, the department must take the following steps. The department is notified of a situation that requires major repair or renovation work. One of the two general foremen visits the site, and "costs out" how much it will cost to do the work. The assistant manager reviews this estimate. If he approves, it is sent over to an accounting department which formally authorizes the maintenance department to undertake the work. As the job proceeds, the foreman keeps a daily log for the production control clerk of the materials requisitioned and the hours spent by various workers on the job. The production control clerk records these amounts in a job file.

The purpose of this record is to allow the accounting department to keep a record of the maintenance department's actual expenditures, which are constantly compared with the expenditures projected

109

in its annual budget. In this process, the department in general and the foremen in particular are working to meet several goals, none of which include the goal of providing the accounting department with an accurate record of the department's activities. The foremen are trying to: accomplish all the necessary repairs, avoid spending more on a job than he originally estimated it would cost, and maintain a high proportion of his crew's labor time charged off against particular jobs. (Work time not spent on particular jobs is counted against departmental overhead). These three goals are also in the interest of the maintenance department as a whole; the conflict is between the maintenance department and the accounting department, not within the maintenance department itself.

For these reasons, the job of production control clerk is transformed from a simple bookkeeping process of recording expenditures into a complex task of working in consultation with the foremen to allocate costs among the various jobs that the department is currently working on. The two general foremen and the production control clerk meet daily to assess the progress of the various jobs, trying to foresee which jobs are likely to come in lower than their original estimates and which jobs are likely to be higher, and shifting their expense accounts around accordingly.

Although a repair job is actually finished when the men have finished the work, it is not officially finished until the cost record is sent from the maintenance department over to the accounting department. The production control clerk and the foremen try to establish a kitty of completed jobs that have come in under their estimates and still have money left in their account which can be allocated elsewhere in an emergency.

Such emergencies occur when the department gets a "call back" on a job. Call backs occur when the repair work fails to solve the original problem or creates new additional problems that must be fixed. Officially the department is supposed to fill out a "supplementary estimate" form on all call backs, a form that must be channeled through the accounting department before the work is done, just like all other estimates. Since the accounting department keeps a record of such supplementary estimates and since call backs reflect badly on the department's work, the maintenance foremen avoid making supplementary estimates whenever possible. They simply do

110

the work and charge it off against some other job that has run under its estimate.

Yet there are still other complicating factors. One of the records kept by the accounting department that is used in evaluating the maintenance department is the length of time needed to officially complete the various jobs. For this reason, jobs that came in under their estimate cannot be kept in the maintenance department indefinitely but must be sent over to the accounting department relatively promptly.

The production clerk finds her work interesting and enjoyable, despite her difficulties with the administrative assistant and her general sense of estrangement from the rest of the office staff. She feels she has almost total control over the records that are used by those higher in the government to evaluate the work of her department and its managers. In her opinion, she and the maintenance men are the core of the department's operations. The maintenance men do the work, the foremen figure out how to do it, and she figures out how to manipulate the paper work to find them the resources they need to get the job done.

In contrast to her relations with the rest of the office staff, she has good working relationships with the maintenance foremen, and she enjoys their daily consultations. They get along well with her and see her as "their representative" in the office. They respect her personally, at least partially because she is the first black woman to reach such a "high" position in the department. (Actually, she earns less than any of the men on the maintenance crew.) They repeatedly tell her how much better she is to work with than the previous production clerks they have experienced, and the sense of appreciation she gets from them at least partially alleviates her frustration at the lack of appreciation on the part of the administrative assistant.

The Mail Room Clerk

The mail room of the main office of a large insurance company takes up one of the below-ground floors in the building. About twenty people work in the mail room, which is divided into two separate operations handling incoming and outgoing mail. Most of the people work in the department that prepares the company's outgoing mail. All bills and other mass mailings from the insurance company are

sent out through this department. The central
equipment in this department are two printers located in a glassed-off corner of the room. Connected
directly to the company's computer, both are kept
operating day and night, printing out bills and
other routine communications that must vary slightly from one customer to the next so that they cannot be printed on normal multilith facilities.

The rest of the department that prepares outgoing mail consists of one supervisor, two mail handlers who lug sacks of mail up the freight elevator to
the loading dock, and eight women who operate a
variety of machines that fold the mail, stuff it into envelopes, seal the envelopes, apply postage and
tie up bundles of envelopes for each different zip
code area.

Every batch of mail sent out has a deadline
attached to it which the mailing department must
meet. The company sends out bills on the 1st, 8th,
15th, and 22nd of every month, or on the last working day before those dates. At these times, the
work is hardest and the pressure most intense.
Between these dates, things are normally more re-
laxed. The morale in this section of the mail room
is relatively high, the deadlines and the pressure
seeming to pull the people together into a cooperating team, and the slack periods in between giving
them a chance to relax and enjoy each other's
company.

The other section of the mail room, where my
informant works, is in charge of receiving the mail
from the post office and distributing it to the
various offices in the building. It also operates
the internal communication system, delivering all
memos and other inter-office communications.

Five men and a supervisor work in this side of
the mail room. The building is divided up, with
each man responsible for approximately three floors
worth of offices. All five men do the same kind of
work and follow the same daily routine. They start
work at eight in the morning, sorting the inter-
office mail that is on hand. Before nine, the morning mail arrives from the post office, and they sort
it also. By ten thirty they are usually ready to
start their morning rounds, finishing the pick-ups
and deliveries before lunch. After lunch, they
start to sort the communications that they have just
picked up. While they are doing that, the second
delivery arrives from the post office, and it also
is sorted. From two thirty until four they make the
rounds again.

This whole routine was instituted by the company a little over a year ago, and it totally transformed the conditions of work of the men in the mail room. Previously, they had no direct supervisor of their own, but were under the nominal supervision of the man who supervises the outgoing mail department. In addition to their corner of the mail room in the basement, they also had assigned to them a closet near the elevators on a middle floor of the building, where they could drop off and pick up mail for each other's departments. They did most of their sorting in the closet upstairs, coming down to the mail room only to pick up the post office mail. They were only expected to deliver inter-office memos once a day, and they only delivered post office mail twice a day to the few departments in the company that regularly receive large quantities of mail.

Those were the golden days of the mail room men, a period remembered fondly. Working basically without supervision, they moved freely about the building, delivering the company's mail for it, but carrying on a great deal of private enterprise at the same time.

The five mailmen are all young, single, and black. They dress boss, talk jive, and walk soul. They cut a wide swath through the insurance company's work force, which is overwhelmingly young, female, white and middle class. Their dropping into an office to pick up the mail is naturally an event that momentarily breaks up the work routine. They try hard to make that event an unforgettable experience, talking outrageous jive and doing their best to bring a little ghetto cool into the mundane lives of these middle class women. Generally this tactic seems to work. Middle class or would-be middle class black women seem to respond with a kind of bemused tolerance, and some middle class white women plainly find them fascinating. I accompanied my informant to a weekly TGIF ritual at a nearby cocktail lounge after work. The group consisted of about thirty young women, eight or ten males (black and white) hanging around the fringes, and four of the five mailmen in the center of the group.

In the golden age before the company reined them in, the mailmen spent eight hours a day moving from office to office, jiving with the women and carrying on their private enterprises. All of the men deal in grass, and one of them can get harder drugs for anybody who wants them. They also market hot TVs, stereos, digital watches, and other consumer goodies that are readily available in the ghetto but not out in suburbia. One of the men also works as a runner for a bookie. The customers must place their bets by phone with the bookie himself, but the mail man will pick up the bets and make the payoffs.

The company cracked down on all this by closing down the men's closet, forcing them to work out of the mail room, and by hiring a new supervisor in an intermediate level of authority between the mail room supervisor and the mail men. For this job, they hired an older black man who was retired from a lower management position in the post office. He instituted the new system that delivers both post office and inter-office mail twice a day to every office in the building. He has also guaranteed the offices that these twice daily deliveries will be made at approximately the same time every day, so that workers who must process the mail will know when to expect to receive it.

This has greatly increased the mail men's work load. Although their new supervisor helps sort some of the mail, since he has no other duties, the switch to twice-a-day deliveries of even inter-office mail to every office has almost doubled the number of stops that they must make. In addition, all these deliveries must now be made within two ninety minute periods in the work day, since all sorting is now done beforehand in the mail room. The sort-first-then-deliver system is not as effi-cient as the men's old method of combining sorting and delivery, but it was instituted as a means of improving social control, not efficiency.

Although the mail men are still able to operate under these new conditions, they have definitely been curbed. They don't have enough time to operate on as large a scale as they used to. They must be much more discrete. Their supervisor knows that they sell grass and take bets for a bookie. This is in line with his previous experience at the Post Office, and he appears to find it acceptable. He is old enough and middle class enough to be bothered more by the jive act that they put on for the white women. They gleefully recount the lecture he once gave them calling this behavior a "disgrace to the race." Moreover, they believe, he would get them fired without hesitation if he ever found out that they also sell hard drugs or stolen goods. All but one of the men have more or less stopped doing this, therefore, since they still feel that they have a good thing going even under the new work conditions and they want to keep it that way.

The Copy Machine Operator

This man works in the central copy department of a government agency devoted primarily to the conduct of applied research. The central copy department is equipped to perform a wide variety of copying jobs that involve either unusual processes or large quantity production. The separate departments in the agency have their own copying machines which they use for the routine production of a few copies of short items.

Six people work in the copy department, a middle aged white woman who is the working supervisor, a middle aged black man who operates various photographic reproduction equipment, and four young people in their twenties. The department is half male, half female; half white, half black. Together, these six people operate a large assortment of equipment. The major items that are in almost constant use include: an IBM copy machine, a Xerox copy machine, a mimeograph machine, a multilith machine, two automatic collators, and a camera that copies to and from microfilm. Additional auxiliary equipment includes: a jogger, power staplers, a power punch, a paper cutter, and a plastic-binding machine.

Although the division of labor in the department is flexible, depending on the work that needs to be done, the workers have their own work stations where they normally spend most of their time. My informant operates the IBM copier and its attached automatic collator. This machine is set up for the rapid reproduction of large numbers of multi-page documents. The Xerox copier is normally operated by one of the women in the department. It can reduce or enlarge originals and produce higher quality copies of photographs or colored originals. This machine has no attached collator. A second woman operates the mimeograph machine, the multilith press, and the machine that makes stencils from typewritten originals. The older man is in charge of all the microfilm and other photographic work. Mostly, this job involves making copies from microfilm originals or making microfilm copies from manuscript originals, but the camera is also capable of making positive or negative copies on film or paper of any original. Another man in the department runs the automatic

collator, the jogger, the staplers, the punch, the
plastic binder -- preparing the work that has been
run off on the printing and copying machines. The
working supervisor spends most of her time helping
out with this work but she is also responsible for
logging in all job orders, checking to see if the
order is signed by the person in each department who
is authorized to do so, scheduling the work, and
filling out the paper work that is necessary so that
the costs of each job can be charged off against the
proper department.

Having worked there for less than two years, my
informant is the junior member of the department.
His job, the operation of the IBM copier, is the
most routinized of any of the jobs in the department.
Every job that he handles involves the multiple
copying of large numbers of 8-1/2 x 11 typewritten
pages. The only variation from job to job is in the
content of the work that he is copying, a variable
that does not affect him at all. Even if he were
interested in reading what he was copying, the IBM
copier (unlike the Xerox machine) must be fed last
page first if the pages are to come out of the
collator in the proper order.

Since the department has a maintenance contract
on his machine, he is not expected to know anything
about it other than how to keep it supplied with
paper and toner. Nevertheless, the half-day delays
that are usually necessary to wait for the company's
repair man are often inconvenient. For this reason,
he watches the repair man at work. Now when something goes wrong with the machine that appears to
him to be a repeat of a previous malfunction, he
sometimes tries to imitate what the repair man did.
Two or three times so far this has been successful,
and he has been able to get the machine working
again without calling in the repair man.

His principal technical accomplishment so far,
one that he is justifiably proud of, is a mechanical
connection (made out of a coat hanger) that links up
the copy machine with its collator. About one in
every thousand copies the collator used to skip a
slot. This would become obvious, when at the end of
a job, in addition to the required number of copies
of the document, there would be an extra slot con-
taining, for example, one copy each of pages 17, 33,
and 62. It would then be necessary to go through
all the copies looking for the places where these
pages were missing, a frustrating and time-consuming
task. Other people who had run the IBM machine had
handled this problem by watching that extra slot,

stopping the machine as soon as a page appeared in
it, and checking the top page in each slot in the
collator to see where that extra page belonged. My
informant was not satisfied with this, however, and
persuaded the department head to call in a repair
man from the company that made the collator (at the
department's expense, since the collator is not
covered by maintenance contract) to try and fix it.
The collator repair man blamed the trouble on the
IBM copier. When the IBM man was called in, he said
it was an electronic malfunction in the collator.
After watching both these men, the operator got the
idea that a piece of wire could be used to force the
copying machine to mechanically push the collator on
to the next slot, regardless of whether the electronic sensing device on the collator that was supposed to accomplish this did its job or not. This
works. There is a problem that the piece of coat
hanger occasionally falls out, but if the operator
watches it and makes sure that it is in place, then
everything works perfectly.

     In addition to the knowledge that he is acquir-
ing about the machine, there are a few other techniques that he has developed to maximize the quality
of the copies. There is a knob that can be adjusted
on the machine to help produce clear, dark copies in
spite of varying qualities of originals. There is
also another control within the machine, that is
normally supposed to be operated only by the repair
man, which permits a larger range of variation. He
uses this internal adjustment mechanism when it is
necessary to try to copy work that is already light
from previous copying processes or work that includes corrections or marginal comments written with
blue ink. He has also developed his own specialized
technique for quickly placing each page of the original in the precise place that will result in an
exactly centered copy.

     Basically, though, the operation of the IBM
copier is a highly routinized job, with a minimal
amount of working knowledge. My informant is not
satisfied with it, but he feels that he would be
satisfied with any other job in the department.
This is because his job, in addition to being the
most routinized, is the one that is in most constant
demand. Whereas all the other members of the
department regularly experience periods when the
machine that they normally use is not needed and
they are shifted to help out with some other job on
some other machine, this hardly ever happens to
him.

An additional area of working knowledge, shared
by all members of the copying department, involves
knowledge of copyright laws and the government regulations governing copy work that is performed within
its agencies. The supervisor regularly receives
memos regarding new developments in the procedures
and guidelines that should be followed. She shows
these memos around, and members of the department
take an interest in this aspect of the work, becoming zealous guardians of copyright privileges. They
take pleasure in the opportunity that they occasionally get to legitimately refuse to do work, enjoying
the feeling of being one up on the professionals in
the other departments.

The Computer Operator

The computer that this man operates is the
heart of a government agency charged with regulating
the practices of corporations that fall within its
jurisdiction. These companies must make regular
reports to the agency describing their operations
and demonstrating their continued compliance with a
number of regulations. This data is stored on line
in the computer, forming the raw material for various reports that are compiled by different departments within the agency.
A second source of data is the agency's own internal affairs. Records are kept of every action
taken, all costs and expenses, all routine cases
processed and reports produced, and all personnel.
Still, all of this data processing activity takes up
less than half the time of the computer, and the
rest of the time is allotted to other agencies that
use this computer on a time-sharing basis.
In addition to the main office where the computer is located, the agency has four other offices,
each equipped with its own set of data input and
output devices and connected by data transmission
telephone line to the computer in the main office.
The other departments that use the computer also
have their own remote terminals. This means that
although there are several input and output devices
under the computer operator's charge, much of the
time when he is operating the computer, nothing
visible is happening. Lights on the control panel
indicate to the operator what the computer is doing,
but the actual input or output of data is occurring
in some other part of the country.
The computer operator has held this job for
three years, first on the second shift and now on

the first shift. This is the only computer job he
has ever held. He prepared for it by taking courses
from a commercial school that specialized in voca-
tional training in the computer field. Most of what
he learned there, however, he has never had a chance
to use on this job. The rudimentary training in
computer languages and computer programming that he
received is not needed to be an operator, nor is it
sufficient to prepare him for programming work, at
least in as sophisticated and large scale an operation as the one where he works.

The data processing department in the main
office employs about twenty people: a department
head and his secretary, about a half dozen programmers and program analysts, three operators (one on
each shift), a dozen keypunch operators, and a data
processing supervisor who is in charge of supervising the keypunch and computer operators. The work
force in the department has an unusually egalatarian
distribution among the sexes. About half the programmers are women, the data processing supervisor
is a woman, and there are currently two male keypunch operators.

The job of the computer operator is to tend to
the computer and its assortment of auxiliary hardware, the various card and tape readers, the printers, the disc units, the various data transmission
terminals. On the night shifts, this is normally a
routine task. The schedule is approximately the
same every night, and there are seldom any small
jobs to run, because there are no programmers or
supervisors working at night. The computer operators on the two night shifts now work alone. When
my informant first came to work on the second shift,
there was also a second shift of keypunch operators,
but innovations in data collection and transmission
technology have reduced the number of keypunch
operators necessary. The second shift was eliminated shortly after he came on the job. The night
shift operators work from a schedule developed by
the head of the department. Since the routine type
of programs that are run at night are all stored,
like the data itself, on memory discs, the only
thing the operator must do to start a job is to pull
out of the file a short piece of tape that tells
the computer what program to execute on which data,
and where the program and data are located on the
discs. If the program is to produce output on one
of the devices in the department, then the operator
must make sure that device is turned on, loaded

with the necessary paper or tape, and ready to go.
Aside from running the department's own work, the
operator follows a schedule showing what times the
computer is accessible to the other departments who
share the facility. During those time periods, he
must make sure he has their discs on line in the
disc unit.

The night operators have a list of the phone
numbers of people to call if anything goes wrong,
starting at the bottom with the program analyst or
"troubleshooter" and escalating to the department
head and to a hierarchy of IBM technical representatives beyond him. There is also a list of emergency
procedures to follow in case of fire or power out-
age. But during the years that my informant worked
the second shift, it never was necessary to utilize
any of these procedures or call any of these people.

These things are more lively on the first
shift. In addition to the routine work, there is
usually also a variety of small jobs, one-time jobs,
and experimental jobs using new software techniques.
On the first shift, therefore, there are constant
interactions between the computer operator, the data
processing supervisor, and the programmers. Because
the computer operator has a closer working familiarity with the hardware, and because he used to pass
the time on the second shift by reading the innumer-
able trade publications received by the programmers
and can speak their language, he is occasionally
consulted as the "hardware specialist." He knows
better than anybody else in the department the
capacities of the various pieces of equipment and
the relative amount of time that they are idle or in
use in the department. When others in the department need this information, they turn to him for it.

As a result of the role he has played in these
consultations, he hopes that the department will
take him on as a trainee the next time there is a
vacancy among the programmers. This kind of move up
the ladder within the data processing field used to
be a common experience in the early days of mush-
rooming growth and shortage of trained personnel.
The top program analyst in the department started
that way, learning on the job without ever having
any formal educational training in programming.
This kind of fluidity and mobility is much rarer
now, however. If my informant is permitted to
switch into programming, it will be the first time
that such a move has ever been made in this department. All the present programmers were hired as

programmers based on qualifications already achieved elsewhere, either through work experience or formal education.

The Secretary

This woman has been a secretary in her company since shortly after it was founded ten years ago. For the last six years she has worked as a secretary for the same man, following him up the corporate hierarchy in the traditional way as he has moved from contract supervisor to his present position as executive vice president. The company that she works for carries out research projects, program evaluations, and training programs in the fields of health care delivery, mental health, and community services. All of this work is done under specific contract to various government agencies.

These contracts are of limited duration, a factor which lends instability to the organization, resulting in unusual terms of employment. An overwhelming majority of the work force in the company is made up of professional and para-professional researchers and research assistants. All of these people are hired for the duration of a single contract only. (Normally this is about two years -- frequently one, rarely three.) At the end of that time, unless they are able to bring into the company a subsequent contract in a related field, their association with the company ends.

The remaining employees of the company are called the "overhead staff," because their salaries are paid out of general overhead instead of out of specific contracts. They include two groups: the eight executives in the top levels of the corporate hierarchy, and the approximately fifteen members of the "office staff." This group includes all the employees who are nominally below the status of the professionals and para-professionals: an office manager; three secretaries who work full time for individual executives; ten clerk-typist-receptionists, including three who work in a separate division; and two black men, known as the "messenger boys," who run the copy machine and maintain the offices as well as deliver messages. Except for the office manager and two others, the office staff is entirely black. The ranks of the professionals and the executives, though integrated, are overwhelmingly white.

121

According to the formal authority structure of the organization, all of the members of the office staff fall under the supervision of the office manager. The three private secretaries, however, are not her functional subordinates, since the only interactions they are likely to have with her are in the form of orders and requests that they pass on to her from their bosses. For reasons discussed below, the three clerk typists in a separate division do not fall under the office manager's supervision either. This convoluted juxtaposition of formal authority relations and de facto control is a result of a recent history of power struggles and disputes. The present president of the company won out in these battles, and it is important to note that the office manager is actually his former secretary and present wife, although she does not use his name.

The company was originally founded at the time of the New Frontier by a group of professionals in the mental health field, for whom this was an idealistic as well as a profit-making venture. Its original contracts were exclusively in the field of community mental health, community organization, and community services. The "communities" referred to in those days were the Black communities of the urban ghettoes. Through the days of the war on poverty and the model cities programs, the company prospered and grew fat. In the late sixties, they successfully branched out into the field of drug abuse control, combining many of their original interests with the new flood of money available in the law enforcement and crime prevention areas.

By 1970, however, most of their traditional contract sources had begun to dry up. As Nixon people replaced Great Society Democrats in the upper levels of the various federal agencies, the federal agencies, the network of acquaintances and informal contacts that had sustained the company in earlier years began to break down. There ensued a series of splits within the founding group as different factions proposed different solutions to the dilemma. As a result of all these power struggles, which my informant described to me as a series of conflicts between successive "pragmatist" and "idealist" factions, the company came to be dominated by one man, the archpragmatist who is now president. Only one other member of the founding group remains active in the company as a head of one of its divisions. The others have either sold out

or stopped playing an active role although they continue to hold their shares of the ownership.

At one stage in this power struggle, the company was reorganized into two divisions, a non-
profit subsidiary which handled all the work in the
field of drug abuse and the parent company which
handled everything else. The drug abuse subsidiary
still exists, working with relative autonomy out of
a store front office in a Black neighborhood. Once
the "idealistic" drug abuse people had split off
from the rest of the company, however, there arose
a new dispute between a new faction of idealists
and the company president. The president, whose
background was more strictly in the medical field
than most of the other founders, wanted to get out
of the community services area completely and concentrate the company resources in the area of medical care. Towards that end, the company acquired
through merger a small chain of nursing homes, a
move that was justified in terms of using the company's expertise in health care delivery.

Most of the professionals and many of the
office staff, who had joined this company originally
at least partially out of a sense of commitment to
improving the quality of life in the Black community,
strongly objected to this new direction in the company. Nevertheless, the president continued to
pursue this new direction, ignoring opportunities to
apply for community service contracts and concentrating all the company's "contract development"
work in the medical care field. Over a two-year
period, most of the community services contracts
ran out, and the professionals who were committed
to that kind of work disappeared from the company
scene. An influential minority among the office
staff, however, was more obstinate.

At that time there was no office manager, and
the office staff enjoyed more discretion than they
do now. They stretched this discretion as far as
possible, operating under a set of priorities that
ran counter to the priorities of their superiors in
management. They gave lavish service and encouragement to the few remaining professionals who were
still trying to develop new community services contracts, and they tried as much as possible to sabotage, through a strategy of passive resistance, the
company's efforts to win medical care contracts.
The file clerks "lost" the announcements and correspondence from government agencies setting forth the
technical requirements of forthcoming medical care

contracts. Secretaries "forgot" to remind their
bosses of the various tasks and responsibilities
related to the acquisition of such contracts,
typists "fell behind" the deadlines for the submis-
sion of such contract proposals. Eventually, the
president learned from his wife-secretary the extent
of this activity, yet his initial attempts to crack
down on it were not completely successful. Finally,
he "solved" the problem by reorganizing the corporate structure of his division into five separate
subdivisions, four in medical care fields, one in
community services. Through this mechanism, he was
able to segregate in a separate subdivision all the
people interested in continuing the community services work. Under the leadership of the token Black
vice president, the remaining committed professionals and the most militant half of the office staff
were given autonomy to continue to do their thing.

Although this move was originally perceived as
a victory for the community services faction, it has
turned out to be otherwise. Without any support
from the central company hierarchy, the people in
this division found it harder than ever to secure
new contracts. The division has continued to dimi-
nish in size ever since it was founded. The original eight members of its overhead office staff are
now down to three, and only a handful of professionals remain working on a few small contracts.

This recent history of power struggles and conflicts has put my informant in an ambivalent position. She supported the community services side of
this debate all along, although she never took a
strong enough overt position to lose her job, since
her boss was the president's strongest supporter
among the executives. (He has emerged from this
shake-up as executive vice president in charge of
all the subdivisions except community services,
which has its own vice president.) As her boss
moved up the corporate hierarchy through this series
of shake-ups, she kept getting promotions and salary
increases every time "her side" lost another battle.
This ambivalence is only a part of a wider role conflict that she experiences on her job, however. Off
the job, she talks and acts like the most liberated
women, having and raising children in her own
"female headed household" without ever marrying.
Yet on the job, she functions basically as a "personal servant," relieving her boss of all the mundane details of his life, arranging everything from
writing his letters to buying his anniversary

presents. Yet although she disagrees with her boss philosophically and finds many of the tasks that he asks her to perform vaguely distasteful, she cannot wholly resent him. He is personally a very pleasant man, a nice guy who is easy to work for. In a succession of secretarial jobs, this is the "best boss" she ever worked for, and she is reluctant to leave. Nevertheless, she wishes she could recapture the feeling she used to have when she felt that the work that she did was actually helping people, contributing to the good of society.*

---

*Although she expressed this theme most strongly in her interview, it was also expressed by several others interviewed, including people in the Cone Department, in the Bank, and elsewhere.

Part II
Working Knowledge Analyzed

Introductory Note

The chapters in Part II construct a "sociological account" of working knowledge and its role in
the workplace. It is intended to be an example of
the kind of "effective way of thinking about things"
called for by Whyte (1969, 713 ff). In Whyte's
view, such an effective way of thinking combines
two elements, a "conceptual framework" and a "body
of theory."

> A framework tells us what elements to
> look for and, in a preliminary way, how
> to fit these elements together. In my
> definition, theory is a body of inter-
> related propositions regarding the re-
> lations among the elements specified in
> the framework. (1969, 714)

In these chapters, the "conceptual framework" is
better developed than the "body of interrelated propositions." This is a necessity imposed by the exploratory nature of this research. The data base
includes a variety of work situations. This makes
possible the kinds of comparisons necessary to
tentatively suggest the limiting conditions for
generalizing theoretical propositions.* The sample
of work situations is still much too skimpy, however, to do anything more than suggest the limits
that apply. In particular, any generalizations
made here refer to work in the 1970's under conditions of advanced capitalism in the United States.

----

*This is the principal advantage that the exploratory research
design followed here offers over the more common design for
exploratory research based on the study of a single case.

Whether or not the concepts developed here consti-
tute an "effective way of thinking" about work in
other modes of production in other social contexts
will have to be determined by empirical research.

As a label for the conceptualizations developed
here, I am much more comfortable with the pheno-
menologists' term for theory as a "sociological
account" (Schutz, 1962). Actions and statements of
workers are interpreted as "rational" responses to
work environments, and are explained as "natural"
responses to social structural features of these
environments. Sociologists find these explanations
satisfying because (unlike explanations that rely
on, say, biological or psychological reduction) the
"social structural reductionism" accords with our
understandings of what sociology is and how it is
done.

This sociological analysis first (in Chapter 5)
defines working knowledge and explains its origins
by referring to the job requirements which workers
must meet. The explanation thus begins by treating
working knowledge as the dependent variable and the
organizational structure of work roles -- the
division of labor -- as the independent variable.
Later, after the presence of working knowledge has
been thus explained, attention shifts to its effects
back on the organizational structure. Working
knowledge is thus treated dialectically, or re-
flexively. Chapters 6 and 7 use working knowledge
as an intervening variable to explain such dependent
variables as alienation (Chapter 6) and control
over the work process (Chapter 7). Chapter 8 sums
up the research findings, and Chapter 9 discusses
some of the more controversial aspects of these
findings, with their possible implications for
current political discussions and policy debates.

5. Which Workers Learn How Much, About What, and Why?

Interviewing workers, one is immediately struck by the selectivity of their working knowledge. Each worker had learned about some aspects of the surrounding work environment. Other aspects, though they appear to the outsider to be equally worthy subjects of curiosity, remained unstudied and unexplored. But there is a principle that underlies the selective learning process: unstudied phenomena remain unknown because they do not normally have any practical consequences affecting the worker's ability to carry out his assigned tasks.

A few people are insatiably curious and seem to enjoy learning for its own sake, but for a majority of the workers interviewed, working knowledge is developed only in response to difficulties that occur on the job. The learning of working knowledge is one step in the larger problem-solving practice of work. Workers learn only what they need to know to get their job done.

Since workers only learn what their job requires of them, then the explanations for the content and extent of an individual's working knowledge must be sought in the variables of the social milieu that define the job and its organizational context.*

Job Factors That Determine How Much Workers Learn

Workers "study" some aspects of their work environment, making those aspects subjects of their

_____

*This discussion, like the rest of this work, abstracts from the personalities of individuals, seeking explanations for people's actions and understandings in their present social setting, not in the past social settings that influenced their personality formation.

131

working knowledge, but other aspects remain unstudied. On what basis do workers make these distinctions? All aspects of the work environment that become subjects of working knowledge share three characteristics. Generally, all three characteristics are necessary. If an aspect of the work environment lacks one, it is not studied but remains a part of the background. To merit workers' study, a phenomenon in the work environment must be (1) a variable that (2) recurs with reasonable frequency, and (3) has consequences that affect individual workers as they attempt to carry out the functions assigned to their job.

Constant factors in the work environment fade into the background, becoming part of the social life world of the work place. They are taken for granted by workers with what Alfred Schutz called "the natural attitude." Working knowledge is learned as part of a problem-solving mode -- constant aspects of the work environment are either not problematic or they are not allowed to remain constant.

Of course, every element in the work environment is a potential variable. The work place is a socially constructed reality. Everything within it is a product of the human will, subject to change at any time. Yet the constant factors in the work place appear to workers' natural attitudes as permanet features of the landscape. This is important, because the managers' ultimate power to assign work tasks, choose among available technologies, and control the division of labor allows them to define constants and therefore maintain ultimate control over working knowledge. (See Chapter 8.)

Every work place contains many elements that, although constant, are nevertheless an annoying source of difficulty or unpleasantness. Workers' adjustment to their work situations are often so complete that they cease to notice these sources of difficulty, losing their feelings of annoyance. Occasionally though, some workers achieve a breakthrough that enables them to see ways of transforming these constant aspects of the environment into potentially controllable variables. These break-throughs are rare events, and only a few were uncovered in the course of this research.

In the Cone Department, a machine operator figured out a way to use water from the drinking fountain to produce a higher quality cone edge than the machinery could otherwise turn out. Two tellers in the bank devised an informal filing system to

132

routinize the processing of customers' pay checks
that are received directly from the employers by
mail. This system saves a teller several minutes
each time she processes one of these checks. The
copy machine operator rigged a coat hanger connection between the Xerox machine and its automatic
collator. The device forces the collator to insert
each page in every slot even when the electronic
device that is supposed to regulate this fails to
work properly. Significantly, the workers who
accomplished these break-throughs were in all cases
people respected by their colleagues as especially
"good" workers.

Although these examples may seem trivial, this
development of new knowledge to transform constant
aspects of the work environment into variables is
important. Once this knowledge has been dissemi-
nated to other workers, it becomes part of the
general stock of working knowledge, and workers are
able to routinely accomplish things that were not
possible before. Machine operators' knowledge about
how to compensate for bad paper and how to adjust
"non-adjustable" parts of their machine must have
originated in this way. That workers learn how to
transform constants into variables is significant.
It demonstrates that workers in the course of their
"normal work"* may develop new knowledge that contributes to technological innovation. More importantly, it demonstrates that management's normal
ability to define the constants in the work environment may also be overcome as working knowledge
develops.

While events that recur so regularly that they
may be regarded as constants in the work environment
do not become subjects of working knowledge, neither
do events that occur so rarely that workers
experience them as unique. Singular events are
understood as accidents, unpredictable intrusions
into the work process that need not be studied
because they are not expected to recur again to
make knowledge of them useful. They may cause
serious problems but they remain in the category of
the unpredictable and the unknowable. Individuals
differ, of course, in the degree of fatalism in
their basic world view. One of the characteristics
shared by the workers who their fellows thought

---

*The phrase recalls Kuhn's concept of "normal science," and
the break-throughs that occur are work place analogies to his
"scientific revolutions." (Kuhn, 1970a)

133

were especially bad at their jobs was their tendency to continue to regard as accidents difficulties which other workers feel are knowable -- explainable, predictable, and therefore to some extent controllable. Conversely, especially experienced workers in relatively routinized situations can be valuable because the length of their work experience allows them to see that even rare events may be recurring phenomena and thus subjects of knowledge.

Summing up what has been said so far, recurring variations in the work environment that present a problem for the worker are the stimuli for the learning of new working knowledge. In other words, in the study of the learning process, obstacles to efficient production must be understood as problem-solving opportunities, and therefore as learning situations.

Jobs vary in the range of potential learning situations that they present to the job holder. Several factors condition this variation and determine the knowledge-enhancing potential of different jobs. One of the most important of these factors is the degree of job specialization, defined as the number of production functions assigned to the job. Learning how to carry out each function is in itself a problem-solving opportunity, and each function thus requires its own body of basic working knowledge of the appropriate procedures. This is a commonplace observation, very similar to the statement by Georges Friedmann (1964, 84 ff) to the effect that specialized workers have less chance to realize their potential than "polyvalent" workers.* Earlier theorist-advocates of the technical division of labor were well aware of this problem. Adam Smith wrote:

> The man whose life is spent in performing a few simple operations, of which the effects too are, perhaps, the same or very nearly the same, has no occasion to exert his understanding, or to exercise his invention in finding out expedients for difficulties which never occur. He natural-

---

*He disputes F.W. Taylor on this point. Taylor had disingenuously equated the specialized workers he was creating with specialists, for example physicians and other professionals, who possess specialized knowledge in addition to a thorough generalized training in their trade. (Taylor, 1967)

ly loses, therefore, the habit of such
exertion, and generally becomes as stupid
and ignorant as it is possible for a human
creature to become. . . .
(1937, 734. Quoted in Marglin, 1974.)

Jobs vary as learning situations not only
according to the number of productive functions
that are allocated to them, but also according to
the degree of routinization that has been designed
into each function. In the machine operator's job,
the packing function is more routinized than the
inspection function, which is in turn more routinized than the machine-tending function. Thus,
although most of the operators' physical activity
invovles routine performance of the packing function, most of the working knowledge that operators
acquire involves the machine-tending function.
The body of working knowledge possessed by the
tellers in the bank consists of basic knowledge of
the procedures of many different transactions or
production functions. Yet the body of working
knowledge of tellers appears to be smaller than
that of the machine operators. This is because each
transaction is so much more routinized in the more
bureaucratized organizational setting of the bank.
The tellers' job is less specialized than either
the machine operators' job or the tellers' jobs in
banks prior to the introduction of electronic data
processing. Formerly, tellers in commercial banks
were specialists in a limited number of transactions, and their windows were labeled -- "savings"
or "checking" or "money orders." Now, these
transactions have been greatly routinized, reducing
the total number of tellers necessary to handle the
same volume of transactions and eliminating the
need for such specialization. Tellers now perform
more functions, but need to know less about each
one. The report-preparation function is the least
routinized, and it (like the operators' machine
tending function) therefore requires the development of more working knowledge than any of the other
functions.
The amount of working knowledge required on a
job is therefore largely determined by routinization and specialization. These two factors are
related to the nominal skill level of the job, but
only tangentially. The jobs studied in this research that required the most knowledge were
secretaries, mechanics, and ink men ("skilled"),
longshoremen ("unskilled"), truck drivers and

135

welders ("semi-skilled"). What these jobs have in common is a relative lack of routinization, because the variable nature of their work makes bureaucratization less feasible.* The classification of jobs by "skill requirements" is faulty not only because it underestimates the knowledge required -- no job is literally unskilled -- but also because it fails to accurately measure the knowledge differences between jobs.**

Another aspect of the work situation proved to be a consistent source of difficulty, and thus a normal subject of working knowledge: the necessary interaction between workers in one job category and the people who do other types of work in the same work situation. This study encountered repeated examples where the carrying out of work tasks required cooperation among workers doing different jobs, while aspects of the formal division of labor tended to encourage competition or antagonism that interfered with this necessary cooperation. Techniques to overcome antagonism and foster cooperation thus became a necessary part of the working knowledge of workers in these situations. This phenomenon will be discussed in more detail later; an illustrative example is all that is necessary here. Mechanics who are at work on a repair are constantly being interrupted by operators who request or demand that they stop what they are doing and come work on the operator's machine, which has just "gone down." Mechanics resent these interruptions -- interviews reveal that mechanics consider them to be "the worst aspect of the job" -- and they can get downright surly about it.*** To overcome this difficulty and to enlist the aid of the mechanics, operators have evolved a body of working knowledge about mechanic-manipulation

---

*See Woodward (1965) for the relationship between standardization of product and bureaucratization, and Blauner (1964) for the relationship between standardization and "craftsmanship."

**For a good demolition of the skill concept as used by the Department of Labor, and taken for granted by most social scientists, see Braverman (1974, p. 424 ff.)

***Some sociologists (Eg., Whyte, 1947) may see this situation as an example of role conflicts based on status inconsistency, but an emphathetic observer might note that constant interruptions are annoying no matter what the relative status of the interruptor and interruptee.

techniques and strategies, of which the nurturance of an "image of competence" is perhaps the most important.

The formal division of labor in the work place determines a job's learning potential, therefore, not only by the tasks it assigns, but by the inter- actions it requires with other workers in other job categories. The job specification assigns the worker a variety of material and mechanical problems to be understood and overcome. It also assigns necessary contacts with others in the work place, people whose circumstances and typical responses the worker must also learn to understand and antici- pate.

A final factor that conditions a job's poten- tial as a learning situation is the degree of over- lap between the difficulties presented on the job and the difficulties presented to members of the general public in their everyday non-working life. An extensive body of knowledge is necessary to successfully drive a car, but in American society this knowledge is no longer the specialized prov- ince, as it once was, of chauffers and others that earn their living by driving a vehicle. Although conceptually, knowledge acquired outside the work place and put to work on the job is just as worthy to be considered working knowledge as knowledge that is learned on the job itself, nobody in fact concedes this. Workers themselves, when asked in these interviews, "What kind of procedures do you have to know how to do to be a good (name of job title)?" invariably neglected to include those procedures, such as sweeping, driving, reading, and writing, that are a normal part of their life off the job as well as on it. The only occasional exceptions to this pattern involved procedures that are taught in schools. Obviously, when people are asked "What they know," things they have been taught in schools come to mind more readily than things they have picked up informally. In any case, when working knowledge required by the job is already a part of the workers' previous experience then the job is less of a learning situation for these workers than other jobs which require knowledge that is more job-specific.

The esoteric knowledge required for some jobs is therefore more appreciated and acknowledged than is commonly-held knowledge, even though the con- tributions of the two types of knowledge to pro- duction may be the same. This creates the possibil- ity that job specialization, even if it contributes

137

to a lessening of the working knowledge required,
may result in increased recognition of the specialized knowledge that is involved.

Subject Areas of Working Knowledge

It is time to turn now from an examination of
the job characteristics that condition the learning
of working knowledge to an analysis of the content
of that knowledge. What are the aspects of the
work situation that become subjects of working
knowledge? What do workers need to know about to
carry out their jobs? Generalizing from the working knowledge discovered in this research, all
working knowledge appears to fit into one basic
subject area, knowledge of routine processing procedures, and four supplementary subject areas:
knowledge of variable properties of the materials
or documents processed; knowledge of variable and
potentially manipulable aspects of the equipment
or machinery; knowledge of patterns of client or
customer behavior; and knowledge of patterns of
work behavior of others in the work organization,
especially including managers. Each of these five
subject areas contains a body of working knowledge
that has been developed to cope with the five
aspects of the work environment that this study has
identified as sources of problem-solving stimuli
for workers.

The workers' knowledge about each of these subject areas invariably contains two elements, the
diagnostic and the prescriptive. The diagnostic is
made up of all the background information about that
aspect of the situation that is necessary for workers to ask and answer the question, "What is the
source of this problem?" The prescriptive element
consists of a repertoire of previously tried and
tested procedures or coping techniques that will
(at least partially) solve this problem. After the
problem has been diagnosed prescriptive knowledge
enables workers to answer the question, "How can
this problem be handled?" In the following discussion of subject areas of working knowledge, it
will be therefore necessary to illuminate both the
diagnostic and the prescriptive element of each
area.

Knowledge about routine processing procedures.
The first subject area of working knowledge is the
most basic kind of knowledge on the job: how to
carry out the routine procedures that are necessary
to accomplish the functions that have been assigned

138

to the particular job. For this type of knowledge, the "problems" that must be "solved" consist of the work tasks that have been assigned to each job category by the management decisions that set up the technical division of labor in the work place. In manufacturing and other blue collar situations, these production procedures involve effecting pre-scribed physical changes. In offices, the tasks involve processing procedures which are necessary for administrative personnel to symbolically record and keep track of the company's accomplishments in the physical and social environment outside the office. (Mills, 1951, 189ff.)

Training programs, where they exist, limit the teaching of working knowledge to this subject area. Newly recruited workers are taught the approved procedures for carrying out their tasks. Manage-ment recognizes the existence and even the impor-tance of this basic area of working knowledge. Formal recognition on the part of management sets this subject area apart from the other subject areas, which are only recognized tacitly and in-formally, if at all.

The labeling of this area of working knowledge as "basic" knowledge about "routine" procedures points out another characteristic of this type of knowledge that separates it from the other subject areas. This subject area contains all the basic know-how necessary to routinely accomplish the assigned work tasks. In many jobs, after a more or less lengthy initial learning period, this knowl-edge can be called into play and utilized almost subconsciously. The knowledge is there, it is being used, yet on another more conscious level the mind is set free to think of other things. In fact, the bank tellers report that after they have learned the correct way to count money, stopping to think about what they are doing slows them down and makes them more prone to errors. When all the con-ditions are right, and nothing in the work environ-ment interferes, this basic level of knowledge about procedures is all that is necessary to accomplish the assigned work tasks in a highly productive way.

But conditions are not always right; other factors in the work environment often do interfere. All the other subject areas of working knowledge are made up of knowledge about the problematic aspects of the work situation that often do inter-fere with this routine productivity. The problems that these other areas of working knowledge help

139

solve are periodically recurring obstacles to this
routine productivity; the solutions that they permit
are a return to the productive "normal" situation.
The other four subject areas of working knowledge
are, in a sense, supplementary to this basic
knowledge. This basic knowledge is in constant
use, the supplementary knowledge is only periodically brought to bear as problems arise.

Knowledge about materials or document processed. A supplementary subject area that all the
workers had learned about consists of the critical
variable properties of the materials (or in offices,
the documents) that they worked with. As in the
other subject areas, the knowledge that the workers
learned about their materials is highly task
specific. Each material and each document has
many variable properties, but workers only learn
about those properties that directly affect their
work. The properties of paper that are critical
for machine operators are the moisture and wax
content. Variations from normal wax and moisture
content affect both the operability of their
machines and the quality of their final products.
All of the other variable properties of the
paper -- its porosity, its weight, its chemical
content, for instance -- might be critical variables for other workers in other jobs in the paper-
making industry, but they don't affect the machine
operators at all. Machine operators don't even
notice that these variations exist. For bank
tellers, the critical properties of the checks
they process are signatures, amounts, dates, and
account numbers, more or less in that order. Once
past the teller, signatures cease to be significant
for the other workers in the bank's bookkeeping
department; for some of them, the critical property
is the check's route code, something the teller
never even glances at. In the publishing industry,
the meaning of the words on a page are significant
variables for the copy editor, but insignificant
for the compositor.*

The examples of heightened perceptual accuity
mentioned in the case studies belong to this

---

*When I first dropped back into school after working as a
compositor, I found it difficult to concentrate on reading
assignments because slight printing errors -- small things
that are not even visible to lay people, like dirty mats,
wrong fonts, and sloppy leading -- used to jump off the page
at me, distracting my mind from the content of the words.

category of working knowledge. They are the diagnostic aspect of this knowledge area: knowledge of
discernible variation that allows the worker to see
trouble coming. The prescriptive element -- equally
important to the problem-solving process -- consists
of the repertoire of adjustments, manipulations, and
coping techniques that can minimize the problem and
allow as much as possible a return to routine procedures.

Knowledge about machinery and equipment. As
Warner and Low (1947) and others have pointed out,
the design of a particular piece of production
machinery actually involves the design of a larger
productive system, which includes as a constituent
elements at least the properties of the production
materials and the activities of the machine's
operators as well as the machine itself. Workers'
knowledge about the machines they use is thus an
integral part of a whole gestalt. Workers learn
specific things about each machine part -- how it is
constructed, how it operates, how it can be adjusted -- they also learn what it does. They learn the
effects of each part's movement on the rest of the
machine and on the material being processed. This
knowledge of how a machine operates in its entirety
and in its detail is a crucial aspect of the working
knowledge of people who work with machines -- a
category which in this study included as many office
workers as factory workers.

It is this confident sense of knowing how the
machine operates that allows the workers to adapt
the machine to their own use, adjusting it and
customizing it in ways that the machine's original
designer never intended. This process of adapting
a recalcitrant machine to better serve the needs of
workers is an important aspect of the work life of
the machine operators in the Cone Department. Their
experience in doing this is the source of their
feeling that they control the machine and not vice
versa. Even in the bank, the tellers' use of their
adding machines illustrates this same application of
working knowledge, although on a simpler level.
Tellers don't just use their adding machines to add
with; they use them to create a running record of
their day's transactions. Thus every transaction
is punched into the adding machine, even when there
is nothing to add. They write in their own personal
abbreviations to indicate the nature of the transaction, and the numbers and symbols taken together
form the daily record. The adding machine is thus

141

transformed into a sort of cash register, or even a typewriter that writes only numbers, because that's what they need it for.

Knowledge about patterns of customer behavior. Of all the work situations studied during this research, workers in the bank are the only ones who come in direct contact with customers, and whose work environment is therefore affected by customer behavior. The bank workers developed some knowledge about patterns of customer behavior -- certain customer relations techniques, cyclical patterns of customer activity, the rudimentary customer typology -- but this area of working knowledge seems less important to them than other areas, especially the bank's procedures and its formal organization. Comparison of the knowledge tellers have developed about their customers with the knowledge reported in studies of waitresses (Whyte, 1947), cab drivers (Davis, 1959) and other service workers demonstrates that the body of working knowledge developed by tellers about their customers is considerably smaller than the working knowledge developed about the same subject by these other service workers. This is probably because the structural context of the worker-customer relation in banks is considerably different. The tellers' income, unlike these other tip-dependent workers, does not depend directly on pleasing each and every individual customer. Also as one of the tellers observed, customers don't seem to approach tellers with the same kind of imperiousness ('I am paying for this, so do as I say.') that is often encountered by workers who perform more personal types of services.

Bank tellers do learn a variety of techniques, nevertheless, that allow them to take control of the interaction, or at least to guide willing customers into easily handled transactions. Most important of these techniques, according to one of the tellers, is the seizing of initiative, starting the interaction on an unusually pleasant note. This generally prevents, from all but the angriest customers, the venting of irrelevant complaints or dissatisfactions on the tellers. For instance, in very busy periods, most customers are a little upset at the length of their wait by the time they reach the tellers. There is nothing that the tellers, who are already working as fast as they feel they should, can do about this. Indeed, the time necessary to "cool out" grumpy customers only aggravates the problem. Under these circumstances,

142

tellers use the following technique to minimize hassles:

> Find something about them and make a
> friendly comment, a little compliment,
> right when they first come up with
> their check or whatever.

Knowledge about the formal organization. This subject area of working knowledge includes all the knowledge that workers develop about the workers in other job categories with whom they come in contact, including management representatives. In other words, this is the area of working knowledge which serves as the basis for the role expectations that workers develop of each other. Management's role expectations of workers in their various jobs may be highly influenced by the organization's formal job descriptions, but workers' role expectations of each other are based more directly on observed patterns of past behavior. Workers also develop knowledge about the formal organization as a separate subject in itself. They understand its division of labor, and they understand how this division of labor can operate, almost like an independent force, to pressure people in different job situations to behave in different ways. In the Cone Department interviews, there were plenty of examples where workers in each of the four different job categories (machine operators, material handlers, mechanics, and ink men) complained about each other's role behavior, but each interviewee also understood the pressures on other workers which sometimes caused them to be unresponsive to the interviewee's needs. Through this kind of understanding, workers in the department overcame the obstacles induced by the division of labor and created the necessary arrangements of mutual cooperation and accommodation.

The most extreme example of a worker overcoming the "natural" contradictions induced by the division of labor to reach an accommodation with people in different jobs was discussed by the welder in the radiator shop. The shop was organized on a piece work basis, and since most of its jobs involved relatively short runs, the time study men were always coming out on the floor to run the times that they needed to figure out pay rates on upcoming jobs. The welder, who was also the union's shop committeeman and could in no sense be consider-

ed "a company man," had developed a pattern of
accommodation with these people:

> We get along all right. See, what they
> like about me is that I give them a good
> time. They always say, 'Jimmy, you gave
> us a good time.' (Q: What is a 'good
> time'? What does that mean?) Even,
> like. That's what they need. Steady,
> so each job takes the same time. See,
> they come to me, they've only got to
> time it through a couple of times, be-
> cause I give them the same readings
> right through, every time. That's the
> way they have to have it, they have to
> have it so it's consistent.

These industrial engineers, trained to believe that
reliability was an accurate indicator of validity,
felt satisfied that they had an accurate timing
for the job if their different readings all came up
with substantially similar results. This enabled
them to finish the timing sooner, and it gave them
the data they needed to show to their superiors
that they had in fact developed a "good" rate.
   By realizing their situation, the welder was
able to meet their needs without sacrificing his
own. He simply developed his own internal timing
mechanism to the point where he was able to work
steadily and maintain consistency. Of course, like
all others workers in such situations (cf. Roy,
1952, 1955), he followed entirely different procedures when he was being timed than he did when
he actually carried out his normal production.
Following all the approved methods and safety precautions to the letter, he could present the appearance of working hard and relatively rapidly during
the timing process, and he could still come up with
a time considerably in excess of what he needed to
do the work comfortably when using the alternate
short cut procedures which he had developed.
   In this example, the welder was able to avoid
conflict by using his knowledge of their work situation to manipulate the time-study men to achieve his
intended result, a comfortable piece rate. This
area of working knowledge is more highly developed
by workers in subordinate positions, who need to
know a lot about the work situations of the
organizationally powerful in order to secure their
superior's witting or unwitting cooperation. People

higher up in the hierarchy do not acquire such
detailed knowledge about the work situation of their
subordinates because they do not view the securing
of their subordinates' cooperation as a problem.
As was stated at the beginning of this chapter,
aspects of the work environment that are not perceived as problems do not become learning opportunities.

6. Workers' Knowledge and Workers' Alienation

All theological or ethical or social scientific
theories of alienation, including the one developed
by Marx, still retain a common element which derives
from their root in the Latin word alienus, an adjec-
tive used to describe something that belongs to
another and not one's self. This common element is
their reference to a process of separation of the
individual from someone or something else. In theological theories one is separated from God or from
the Geist. In various social scientific theories
one is separated from society, or the state, or
one's former property or one's own activity, or from
some aspect of one's personality or self. All these
theories of alienation carry the explicit or implicit assumption that the particular separation that is
referred to should not have occurred. In theological theories the separation is seen as contrary to
God's will or to natural law and, therefore, evil
or immoral. In social scientific theories the separation is seen as contrary to some postulated
vision of nature or human nature and, therefore, un-
healthy or socially pathological. (Compare Schacht,
1970).

The Marxist theory of alienation refers to a
collection of separations and estrangements that
result from the defining structural conditions of
capitalism: the separation of workers from control
over their product, which results in workers losing
control over necessary means of production, which in
turn forces workers to sell their labor power to the
owners of those means of production, the capitalists. These separations are pathological because
work ceases to be the source of human progress, the
activity in which man "develops his slumbering
powers," (Marx, 1967, 177) and work becomes instead
a stultifying, mind-destroying mechanical activity.

147

Further, alienated workers not only fail to develop their own potential, but their work does continue to develop the potency of capital, thus adding to the social relation which is the cause of their alienation in the first place.

In Marxist theory, alienation has an objective source in the capitalist social structure. Insisting on this, Marxists have delivered polemics against social-psychological theories of alienation. However, in their indisputably correct assertion that workers do not just "feel" alienated but have in fact sold (literally alienated in the still-Latinate legal sense) their labor power to their employers, Marxists have tended to neglect the equally important subjective aspects of the theory. Alienation is a central concept for Marx's critique of capitalism because the objective condition -- sale of labor power -- has a subjective result, the stifling of the human potential of the laborer. This subjective process, the limitation of the biographical development of masses of individuals, has in turn an objective consequence of its own, the stifling of the historical development of the human species.

The objective and subjective aspects of the alienation concept are thus linked into a single dialectical whole. It makes no more sense for contemporary Marxists to exclude the subjective aspect than it did for Seeman (1959) to attempt to exclude the objective aspect. The present discussion of alienation will attempt, therefore, to use Blauner's (1964) four aspects of alienation -- powerlessness, meaninglessness, self-estrangement, and isolation. Blauner's concepts are used here (though I reject Blauner's operationalizations of them) because all four are indeed alienating negations of human well-being, as that well-being is understood by the mature Marx in his magnum opus, Capital (1967, Chapters I-III, VII).*

---

*This obviously controversial effort to reinvigorate the social-psychological aspects of Marxist theory reflects my belief that Marxist sociology must develop a micro-level complement to its macro-level theory if it is ever to become capable of addressing the whole range of the discipline's concerns. This is not the appropriate place for a theoretical essay justifying the necessity and practicality of a micro-level Marxist sociology, but nevertheless readers should be aware of my belief in the need for such a fully sociological Marxist approach.

Blauner has made the comment that the alienation concept is problematic because it "promises too
much." He is saying that, at least in the social
psychological sense in which he uses the concept,
there can be no such thing as totally non-alienated
work. (1964, 187)*

The rest of this chapter will attempt to demonstrate a converse of Blauner's position. For him,
the theory of alienation promises too much to idealists and humanists, because it holds out the utopian
promise of a completely non-alienated work situation.
The position taken here is that the traditional alienation concept exaggerates the extent of alienation and the potential for discontent.**

Precisely because alienation is as pathological, as contrary to human nature, as Marx said it
was, workers constantly struggle against it. This
struggle takes the form of constant efforts to
breathe life into work, to take activities and relationships that have been formally established only
as a means to life and to transform them into life
activity into ends in themselves.

It is useful at this point to introduce
Toennies' concepts of Gemeinschaft and Gesellschaft
into the discussion. For Toennies, these were ideal
type characterizations, not of whole societies but
of social relationships, which he called "social
entities." Gemeinschaft and Gesellschaft relationships are distinguished from each other by the in-
tentions of the people in the relationship.
Gemeinschaft relationships are an expression of

---

*See also Berger's concept of the "componential self." He re-
fers to the ability to be objective about one's self and one's
performance, an ability which is only made possible by a certain amount of distance between one's practical activity and
one's inner self. The componential self concept and the self-
estrangement concept both view the same phenomenon, but the
former sees it as a positive utilization of human potential
while the latter sees it as a potential-denying pathology
(1974, 33).

**The argument laid out in this chapter is not in any sense a
variant of any of the traditional arguments against the revolutionary potential of the working class. For instance, there
is no reason to believe that extreme alienation is as likely
to lead to revolutionary discontent as it is to lead to hope-
lessness and fatalism. In fact, in modern Marxist-Leninist
political practice, the revolutionary vanguard is sought in
the less alienated sectors of the working class, the peasan-
try, and the petty bourgeoisie.

"natural will." They are multi-faceted, holistic, emotionally engaged relationships which are entered into as ends in themselves, because of the gratification that people receive as an inherent part of carrying on the relationship. Gesellschaft relationships are an expression of "rational will." They are entered into because of a rational calculation that the relationship can serve as a means toward achieving some end that is beyond the relationship itself. (Toennies, 1957)

People enter into work situations primarily as an expression of rational will. For both employee and employer, the relationship is an instrumental one: for the employer it is an investment in variable capital, for the employee it is a means to gain access to the wages necessary for subsistence. In fact, during Toennies' lifetime, the German word Gesellschaft referred primarily to a business firm, a company or corporation. It is fair to say that the employment relationship is the kernel which gave rise through a process of generalization to the Gesellschaft ideal type. Once at work, however, people begin to transform the original Gesellschaft social relations into Gemeinschaft relationships. This process of change from Gesellschaft to Gemeinschaft is depicted in Toennies' writings as a direction of social change which is just as likely as the more famous evolution from Gemeinschaft to Gesellschaft. The process of transforming instrumental actions and relations into valued ends in themselves affects the alienation of workers in all four of the Seeman-Blauner senses of the concept (self-estrangement, social isolation, meaninglessness, powerlessness).

In all of the work situations studied, with the single exception of the office of the production control clerk,* workers who were brought into face-to-face contact by the technical requirements of their work tasks transformed these relations from Gesellschaft to Gemeinschaft relations. This behavior may be a result of inate human needs, as Maslow (1954) and Slater (1970) suggest, or it may be the result of a universal tendency toward goal displacement (Merton, 1968). In any case, it is also a response to work task requirements. The division of labor in these work situations frequent-

---

*See Chapter 4, where the description of this work sitaution also advances an explanation for this anomaly.

150

ly resulted in situations where the short-term
interests of individual workers came in conflict
with their own and others' long-term interests. The
momentary convenience of one worker must be sacrificed or the result will be greater inconvenience
for others. The transformation of these interactions from formal cooperation to Gemeinschaft mutual
help makes it easier to sacrifice short term self-
interest and therefore also serves the requirements
of production.*

Working Knowledge, Work Communities, and Alienation

The fact that communal networks act to reduce
social isolation is a trivial tautology, based on
the definition of the social isolation concept. The
means by which communal networks and working knowledge act to reduce powerlessness, on the other hand,
is a complex and interesting set of phenomena;
it is analyzed separately in the next chapter. The
discussion in this section will focus on the impact
of networks and knowledge on meaninglessness and its
corollary, self-estrangement.
These are the two most social psychologistic of
the four concepts. Powerlessness and isolation are
objective "social facts" (Durkheim, 1950) which
exist in the social world external to the individual. Like any other aspect of the social environment, they can be studied as social psychological
variables, by shifting the subject of analysis, as
Seeman proposed, from the real social relations
themselves to the individual's perception of these
relations. The concepts of meaninglessness and
self-estrangement, on the other hand, are properties
of individual mental states. Meaningful-meaningless
is an attitudinal dimension describing an individual's perception of any phenomenon or event. The
alienation theory applies this attitudinal dimension
to the individual actors' perceptions of their own
activity. The state of alienated meaninglessness
exists to the extent that the actors believe that
their own activity is inconsequential (literally
without consequence) because the effect of the
activity is not known to the actor. Since work

---

*The working out of these potential conflicts of interest
within the work community involves continual griping, com-
plaining, and argument -- overt conflict that, as Simmel
noted, reveals the underlying cooperation (Simmel, 1950)

activity in its most abstract sense -- the effort to transform nature to meet human needs -- is according to Marx (1967, Chapter VII) the defining characteristic of humanity, people unable to see the meaning of their work would indeed become estranged from a fundamental aspect of their human existence.

Self-estrangement is used by the alienation theorists in two senses, one of which is a direct corollary of the meaninglessness concept, and the other of which is not. Usually, self-estrangement is used to refer to the alienated state of being of a person who is engaged in "meaningless" activity. An expanded version of the self-estrangement concept, for instance, the one used by Mills in his discussion of white collar workers (1951, 182 ff), refers to any self-distancing from one's role-required activity, for instance, the way in which salesmen "package" aspects of their real personality and use them instrumentally to promote sales.

The establishment of communal networks and the learning of working knowledge are two strategic approaches to the work context that tend to de-alienate the work. Both networks and knowledge are instrumentally necessary to workers. Both are required to get their job done. Despite this instrumental origin, however, people in all of the work situations studied had "displaced" both working knowledge and communal networks into ends in themselves. The network especially had been transformed from an association necessary to get the work done to an end in itself. Frequently it seemed that the work was done to participate in a communal network rather than vice versa. For a few of the people interviewed, it also seemed that the learning of working knowledge had also become an end in itself. For these people, the knowledge they had acquired and their attitudes toward it bring to mind such concepts as Veblen's "instinct of workmanship." (1914)

The answers to some of the questions asked in the formal interviews can serve as indicators of the importance of the communal networks and working knowledge in the work situations studied. Almost all of the workers in both the Cone Department and the Bank answered that the other people they worked with were the "best aspect of the job." "Try to get along with the others you work with," was listed as the most important work goal by a plurality of the workers interviewed, and it was "also important" to many others. This was the highest rated work goal of any of the options offered. The only other

work goal that was mentioned as often was, "Try to
learn as much as you can about the work, so you can
handle the problems that come up." This was mentioned usually as an "also important" goal rather
than as a main work goal.* Overall, these two work
goals were in a high-rated class by themselves.

The workers' transformation of working knowledge and communal networks into ends in themselves
enables them to considerably reduce their own alienation in the work situation. Through their learning
of working knowledge and through their creation of a
communal network, workers invest their own work
activity with meaning. As described in the previous
chapter, the whole of an individual's working knowledge constitutes a paradigm which the worker uses
to understand her work situation and her position
in it. This paradigm synthesizes the individual
elements of their working knowledge into a "cogni-
tive map" (Holzner, 1972, 20 ff.) which explains
phenomena in the work situation contextually. This
contextual explanation involves knowing how things
in the work situation normally interact to build
chains of mutual causation or determination. The
paradigm allows the worker to understand any particular event in terms of its probable causes and its
predictable consequences. In the same way, the
paradigm allows the knowledgeable worker to understand the contextual meaning of her own acts.

In the break-in period after the end of the
formal training and before the worker has been able
to reconstruct the individual items of working knowledge into a holistic paradigm, it is true that the
worker's activities are meaningless. She is doing
what she has been told to do in the training period,
but she has not yet reconstructed the reason why
the work must be done in this prescribed way. Workers in both the Bank and the Cone Department reported that in the beginning, "nothing made any sense."
After the acquisition of the paradigm, however, the
worker does understand how her work actually meshes
in with the work activity of others and what the
consequences would be for these others should she
deviate from the prescribed procedures. This knowl-

_____

*The rating of this second work goal must be considered to be
artificially inflated to an unknown extent by the contextual
effect of the interview, since the question on work goals
was asked toward the end of an interview that had focused
itself primarily on the issue of working knowledge.

edge gives her the freedom to adapt her work activity and develop her own personal methods, based on her paradigmatic understanding of the work.

In addition to providing work activity with a meaning based on the internal context of the work situation, working knowledge also provides an interpretation of the reality external to the work organization, an interpretation which also helps to render work activity meaningful. All the workers interviewed had developed their own idea of the concrete use value of their work, why it was useful, what it was useful for, and who it was useful to. This was not just a general, theoretical viewpoint about why their work was important. (Occasional management attempts to impress workers with the social importance of their particular work as a morale boosting measure were viewed with cynicism and derision.) Rather, this understanding of the concrete use value of their work served as a realistic guide in day-to-day decision making. In the Cone Department, the machine operators know what their cones are used for, and they know how the consumers use them. This knowledge serves them daily as they make their decisions about which substandard cones to sneak by the inspectors and which ones to discard. Tellers in the Bank, since they are also members of the general public themselves, put themselves in the place of their customers and take the unspoken desires of the customer into account when making small decisions about appropriate procedures to follow in each different transaction. Even on the automobile assembly line, which Blauner (1964), Ritzer (1975), and others consider to be the ultimate of alienated work situations, the worker at each station along the line knows exactly how his activity affects the ultimate use value of the automobile.

In situations of really extreme potential meaninglessness, where the useful purpose of their work is actually not known to the workers themselves, working knowledge can help create dimensions of hypothesized external utility. An extreme example of this type of potentially alienating situation can be seen in a plastics factory, where women in the molding department ran machines that stamped out assorted black plastic parts used in the aerospace industry. Since the women had no idea what these parts were, or what each part might be used for, they had no real way of knowing what characteristics of the finished product would increase or decrease the usefulness or quality level of the product. They solved this problem by assuming that mold marks

154

and rough edges, which detract from the appearance
and feel of the product, would also detract from its
utility. They therefore concentrated their quality-
enhancing activity on these product characteristics.*
     This understanding of the utility of the work
they put out, of the purpose of the consumer, is a
key element on which the whole paradigm of working
knowledge rests. It forms the underlying basis of
all quality standards, and it allows workers to set
priorities in their work, assessing the ultimate
importance of the various work tasks that make up
their job. The goal of trying to "put out the highest quality work that you can" received the third
highest overall rating in this study, and was important to workers in all of the work situations. The
importance of quality work is especially noticeable
in comparison with the quantity-maximizing goal
which was the second most negatively rated goal in
the whole study.
     In general, this research found no support for
Marx's statement that:

     In fact, of course, this 'productive'
     worker cares as much about the crappy
     shit he has to make as does the capi-
     talist himself who employs him, and
     who also couldn't give a damn for the
     junk." (1973, 273)

While this statement may be applicable to the un-
employed worker who is looking only for "a job" and
who would be willing to do anything as long as the
wage rate is adequate, once at work and actually engaged in the process of concrete labor, workers
appear to take very seriously the social responsibility of producing the particular use value to
which they are assigned.
     This serious dedication to concrete work tasks
is reinforced by the workers' participation in the
communal network. The quality production of use
values takes on an extra dimension of meaning within
the communal network. Fellow workers expect each
other to do their share and participate fully in the
necessary work. Knowledgeability and proficiency
and the performance of high quality work are respected attributes. In all of the work communities
studied, the people in each community who were most

_____

*Thanks to Eileen Berger for providing this example of her
former work situation.

155

respected and most liked were invariably also "good
workers." This is a necessary but not sufficient
condition for esteem among the workers in those situations. All the people who were unusually well respected or liked by their fellow workers were "good
workers"; all "good workers" were not necessarily
liked or respected, however. Good workers who
appear to their fellow workers to be motivated by a
desire to impress or "suck up to" management were
generally scorned rather than esteemed.*

Learning about their work and participating in
their communal network, workers are able to self-
define their work activity as meaningful activity
which is intrinsically worth-while and not simply a
drudgery necessary to earn a wage. At some point in
each interview, every worker in this study made some
kind of statement that expressed an implicit commitment to the work as a meaningful end in itself. In
these moments, the workers demonstrate a commitment
to, and immersion in, their jobs which indicates the
extent that they have been able to overcome self-
estrangement to transform their work activity into
life activity. The following quotes will give a
sense of the way workers express this non-alienated
commitment:

> I mean if I'm going to be a machine
> operator, then I've got to be a good
> one. I can't be a good person with-
> out being a good machine operator.
> (Machine operator, cone department)

> Of course, it's such a filthy job, being
> an ink man. You've got to love it, or
> you couldn't do it....I'm proud of it,
> I'm good at it. (Inkman, cone department)

> Well, tellers are what the bank is
> about, really. We're the ones that

---

*"Suck up to" was the sexual metaphor generally used by almost
all workers. In the warehouse, workers who made a regular
practice of this activity were called "popsickle men," or even
"pink popsickle men." This phrase expresses the basic metaphor even more vividly, and in the latter version also points
out the racial stratification that prevailed in that particular work situation. Interestingly, male workers were much
more tolerant of this practice among female fellow workers
than they were of fellow males or than female workers were of
each other.

156

actually help the customers out,
give them the service....We get
people in here with their accounts
in all these other branches. They
go out of their way to come over
here, because of the service we
give....You can't help but feel good
about it. (Teller, branch bank)

You run a smooth bead, you can see
it, you know. You do quality work,
and you know it. Anybody else
comes along, they know it too.
(Welder, radiator shop)

The Conflict Between Concrete Labor As An End And Abstract Labor As A Means To Profit

In the communal networks of the management personnel, there occurs a reversal of concrete and abstract labor. Workers in capitalist firms carry out
abstract labor -- that is, they produce exchange
value for their companies -- but they do so only as
a consequence of concrete labor -- that is, the
particular work tasks that produce a particular use
value. On the other hand, all the concrete work
tasks of management -- planning, scheduling, coordinating, supervising, evaluating, cost-monitoring--
contribute mainly to the production of exchange
value. That is, they abstract from the concrete
tasks that produce particular use values. This is
readily evident from talking with managers* or from
reading management texts. Managers see their jobs
as "working with people" and they expect that good
managers can move from department to department,
company to company, even industry to industry without decreasing the effectiveness of their managerial
work. Because of this aspect of their work role,
and because of their participation in a managerial
communal network that closely identifies their own
welfare with that of the company, as measured by the

---

*One of the reasons that Hughes (1958) advocates the study
of "low status" workers is that "high status" workers can
discuss their work only in terms of glib abstractions.
The unsatisfacotry interviews that result make it hard for
sociologists to study actual behavior except by lengthy
and expensive participant observation. My students and I
have been frustrated by this problem in other research
projects.

yardstick of profitability, managers above the rank of first-line supervisors continue to view concrete labor primarily as a means, and not as an end in itself.

This difference in outlook between the managers and the workers is a constant source of conflict. Managerial policy decisions create formal organizational structures, work roles, particular work tasks, all called into existence only as means to a particular end, the maximization of profit. Yet these are the very factors which become the social life worlds of workers, the subjects of their working knowledge and the specialized milieu in which their communal networks are effective. In the process of de-alienating their work, workers transform these artifacts of managerial policy decisions into indispensable settings for life activity.

Yet from the management point of view these organizational aspects of concrete work situations originally came into being only as a means of profit maximization, and their continued existence is contingent upon their continued service as profit enhancers. If market conditions outside the firm change, these formerly profitable arrangements may become less profitable or unprofitable. When this happens, the company must move with the times, the management must reorganize itself, either by producing the old use values in a more efficient new way or by moving into the production of altogether different new use values. These changes are not problematic for management, because managers have been abstracting from concrete labor all along, and their communal network has not transformed any of these organizational arrangements into ends in themselves.* Such changes are extremely significant to workers, however. Without even thinking in these terms or realizing what it is doing, management can render whole subjects of working knowledge obsolete, disrupt communal networks, and thus undermine or eliminate entirely the resources that the workers have used to render their jobs meaningful and to turn their work activity into life activity.

Naturally workers resist such changes. From this defensive resistance, and the conflict that results, management forms a view of workers as anti-progressive, anti-technology, anti-change. This is not necessarily the case. Both paradigms of working

_____

*This is probably an exaggeration, justifiable only as an "ideal type" contrast to the attitudes of workers.

knowledge and communal networks have their own
internal dynamisms. Both are constantly growing,
developing, and contributing to change in the work
situation. These internal dynamisms are the source
of much of the innovation in the work places studied
here. The new more efficient methods worked out by
material handlers, machine operators, and bank tellers are all examples of this. The most spectacular
example is the new type of "light" cone machine
developed by the mechanics in the Cone Department,
whose growing body of working knowledge eventually
led to the designing of a new machine incorporating
significant technological break-throughs. In
capitalist firms, where all legitimate policy-making
authority rests with management, working knowledge
and communal networks remain basically responsive,
coping mechanisms. There is no reason why they
could not also serve as change agents, but in
capitalist firms this is normally not legitimate.

When these conflicts arise between the managerial community's means orientation and the workers'
community's ends orientation, management perceives
the problem as the workers' inability to see "the
big picture." Management feels that it has an overview of the whole company's operation, a picture
which comes from access to various statistical and
other summarizing measures and reports. Workers in
particular departments do not have this kind of
overview, but they feel that management lacks a
necessary familiarity with the particulars of their
work sitaution, and that this unfamiliarity prevents
management from making rational decisions about the
particular department. An ironic aspect of the
difference between these two world views is the
possibility that the workers' use value orientation,
rooted in the concrete details of particular work
practices, may actually be "the bigger picture" if
we look at this conflict from the point of view of
the society outside of the company.* From the outsider's perspective, it is just as suitable to view
the workers' world view as the more inclusive one,

_____

*This is the only reasonable way to look at it. The
debates in the organizational literature about who or what
is "rational" dissolve into nothingless unless they spec-
ify what end (and whose!) the rationality serves. From
the point of view of the whole society, the "rationality"
of production organizations must be assessed in terms of
the socially necessary production function in which they
are ostensibly engaged.

since their concern is with producing the use values needed by the society, while the management may disregard social needs in its focus on the individual company and its profitability.

In another sense, the management view is usually seen as the more realistic, because its focus on changing market conditions is necessary if the company is to continue to show a profit, stay in business, and provide the workers' jobs. Yet one might dispute this view of managerial "realism." Perhaps this focus on the production of surplus value instead of use value is really "surrealistic," as implied in Marx's theory of the fetishism of commodities. (Marx, 1967, 71 ff.)

Yet if management's view is actually the more unreal, this surrealism pervades the whole society, and affects workers' families as well as management. Once they have left the job and the work community, these workers are faced with an attitude on the part of family and friends that refuses to accord legitimacy to their use value orientation or their transformation of their jobs into ends in themselves. In this society, people who are neither executives nor professionals nor self-employed are not expected to treat their work as anything other than a means to earn a living. To families and friends off the job, events in the work place are essentially without intrinsic interest. Workers are not expected to "bring their jobs home," a requirement that forces workers to deny at home the very meaningfulness which they have painfully created for themselves at work.

The legitimacy of their use value orientation and their Gemeinschaft work relations is continually therefore being undermined, both by management on the job and by family and friends off the job. This has serious consequences which leads workers to adapt an attitude that can only be described as a kind of fundamental ambivalence. Since the value of their de-alienating working knowledge and working relationships is continually denied by people in formal positions of authority on the job and by respected peers off the job, workers are in a state of constant vacillation between active de-alienation and passive acceptance of alienation. An idea of the pervasive quality of this fundamental ambivalence might be indicated by the following quotes, which come from the same interviews with the same workers as the four cited earlier as examples of non-alienated commitment.

160

They (management) pull a stunt like
this, you say to yourself, for two
seventy-five an hour, why bust my
ass? (Machine operator, cone department)

When you work in a factory, you can't
put your whole self into a job. The
man in the office, he only wants to
make money, he doesn't care.
(Inkman, cone department)

A money-counting machine, that's all
they want basically. If you just
counted the money right, didn't put
anything else into it, that would be
all right with them. (Teller, branch
bank)

Do you show up every day, that's all
they care about. Welder, sheet metal
-- any job, it doesn't matter -- as
far as they're concerned, if you show
up in the morning on time, you're doing
good work. (Welder, radiator shop)

All the workers interviewed in this study were
alienated workers. But the alienation that they
express in these interviews is a very subtle thing.
They have invested a lot of energy in de-alienating
themselves, in learning the working knowledge and
building the work relationships that add to their
own control over work processes, decreases their
social isolation, and make their work meaningful.
Through this de-alienating effort, they deny and
affirm their own alienation at the same time. They
struggle against it, but at least in the context of
capitalist work organizations embedded in a capitalist society they cannot overcome it. In the final
analysis, then, the alienation is not the powerlessness, meaninglessness, etc. but the lack of an
institutional framework that would recognize and
legitimize the knowledge and communal relations
which can so effectively combat these things.

161

7. Working Knowledge and Work Control

Working knowledge, like other cultural forms, is a mode of adaptation on the part of workers to their work environment. Unlike some other forms of cultural adaptation -- extreme self-estrangement, the use of drugs or alcohol to put mental distance between one's self and the environment -- the learning of working knowledge is a mode of adapting to the work place which increases the worker's ability to be effective in that environemnt, to manipulate it, or even to transform it.

Early in the Cone Department study, two of the workers interviewed expressed the idea that the knowledge being talked about was really "survival knowledge." The two workers used the concept of survival knowledge in slightly different ways. To one, this know-how was necessary to get along with one's fellow workers, to perform up to their expecttations and, therefore, to secure their help and cooperation when needed. For the other worker, this know-how was necessary to survive in the sense that "otherwise, you'd go crazy." This machine operator went on to create an image of what it would be like to work in a situation where the old machines break down, the substandard paper acts up, the material handler is never around when you need him, and the mechanic won't help at all. How could anybody survive in such a world without knowing enough about the physical and social environment to be able to predict these occurrences, to prepare for them, and perhaps even to prevent some of them? Another machine operator had this to say:

> I run that machine. It doesn't run you, you run it. I mean, some of these oper- ators -- you don't know what you're doing, the machine's going to run you,

163

that's right, no question. You been
there as many years as me, though, you
know what you're doing, you know how to
do it right, then you run that machine,
it doesn't run you."

In the bank, one of the tellers used these
words to describe the head teller, who is generally
considered by the other tellers to be the "best
teller" at that branch:

She knows everything there is to know
about the bank: all the policies, the
other departments. She never has to
lose her cool with a customer. She
knows what's right, she knows what to
tell them, and she tells them, and
that's it. She's very professional.

Working knowledge helps workers survive in the
work environment because it enables them to understand the social and material forces shaping the
environment, to explain the things that happen to
the workers, and even in some cases to predict
some of these things. This understanding lays the
basis for the worker's feeling that she is in control of the environment, that she is competent, and
that she can handle whatever happens to her. There
is an issue here of how much the possession of working knowledge truly enables workers to actually
control the environment and how much it merely
enables them to feel in control. There is an
element in the machine operator's statement about
her relation with her machine that seems to protest
too much. Yet, the evidence from the case studies
support the interpretation that the workers are,
because of their know-how, in fact effective. Most
of the time the operators are in fact able to get
both machines and fellow workers to obey their will.
In the bank, the tellers by and large do manage
to control the paper work, avoid settlement
problems, and handle the customers. These workers
do not just feel able to accomplish these things,
they accomplish them.
After the first case study, an additional question was inserted in the formal interviews. Workers
were asked, "Do you think you know more about your
work than management seems to think is necessary
for a person in your position to know?" All but
two workers answered that yes, they thought they did

164

know more. They were then asked why they had learned that "extra" amount of knowledge. In their
answers, the workers generally stressed two themes.
Most said that their own personal standards were
higher than that of management, and the extra knowledge was necessary to live up to these higher
standards. Others gave answers that could be con-
strued as referring to an effort to get better control over their work situation: "It's necessary to
keep things organized around here."* (Bank teller);
"Because it helps me to see what's coming down, and
how to deal with it" (Secretary, contract research);
"To deal with the customers' questions, just to keep
them happy and off your back" (Bank clerk, new
accounts desk). These answers indicate that workers
are at least on some level aware that their learning activity is a form of coping, a means of dealing with the work environment by obtaining some control over it.

In the classic Comteam sense,** working knowledge is a means of increasing the autonomous control of the worker-learner over herself and over
her own activities, which in turn implies -- in
fact, requires -- control over her immediate environment. In the sense that all activities are interactions with the environment, then autonomous
actions are ones that are independently willed by
the actor. In non-autonomous situations, events in
the environment require certain actions and responses from the actor, whose only choice is whether
or not to submit.***

Working knowledge increases the autonomy of
workers because it gives them the tools they need to
diagnose events and situations that arise in the
work place and to prescribe the actions which workers can take to handle these events or situations,
to get them back under control. Workers' knowledge
provide them with a technically informed paradig-

---

*In this case "organized" refers to smoothly functioning
work processes, not to unions or unionization.

**The goal of Auguste Comte's positivist social science was
"to predict in order to control." (See Lenzer's 1975
selection, passim.)

***In this sense, autonomy is the direct converse of Seeman
and Blauner's conceptualization of the "powerlessness"
dimension of alienation. (Seeman, 1959; Blauner, 1964).

matic perspective of their work environments. Workers diagnose events by applying this paradigmatic
perspective to infuse these events with meaning.
The process of understanding these events involves
looking at their context, explaining their occurrence in terms of the precipitating factor that
"caused" them, and predicting their consequences,
the future events that these events will in turn
precipitate. All these elements together make up
the workers' diagnosis of the situation. From this
diagnosis flow certain prescriptions for future
actions that can be taken to control this predicted
sequence of future events. When in the course of
her routine quality-control inspection, a machine
operator comes across a cone with a particular type
of defect, the working knowledge she has and the
paradigm it provides allows her to figure out the
defect's probable causes, to decide whether it
results from a unique quirk or some developing
problem in the production process, and if necessary,
to prevent the problem from developing further.
Tellers' paradigms allow them to track down the
source of settlement errors like a detective searching out a suspect, and to either eliminate the error
(this is possible for errors in calculation) or to
avoid its future recurrence (the only possible
remedy for record-keeping or money-handling errors).
    In terms of their autonomy-increasing capabil-
ity, each of the subject areas of working knowledge
discussed earlier can be understood as aspects of
the work environment which are brought under a
greater degree of worker control through the
possession of working knowledge of that subject
area. Knowledge about the materials or documents
and knowledge about the equipment enable workers
to increase their autonomy over aspects of the
physical environment of their work places. The
other two supplementary subject areas of working
knowledge -- knowledge about patterns of customer or
client behavior, and knowledge about management and
the formal organization -- increase workers' control
over the social environment of the work place.

Working Knowledge and the Craft Administration of Production

    In the process of diagnosing problems in the
work situation and prescribing the actions necessary
to resolve them, workers are acting as their own
decision makers. Stinchcombe (1959) has contrasted

166

"bureaucratic" and "craft administration of production." His main thesis:

> is that the professionalization of the
> labor force in the construction industry
> serves the same functions as bureau-
> cratic administration in mass production
> industries and is more rational.
> (1959, 168)*

Stinchcombe argues that under conditions of economic instability and technological variability, craft administration is the more rational system because it reduces overhead. For Stinchcombe, bureaucratic and craft administrations are alternative types. The bureaucratic type predominates in mass production and the craft administration type in the construction industry -- and presumably other industries where a unit production predominates (cf. Woodward, 1965). Because of this product variability,

> Decisions, which in mass production were
> made outside the work milieu and communi-
> cated bureaucratically, in construction
> work were actually part of the crafts-
> man's culture and socialization, and were
> made at the level of the work crew...(and)
> the legitimate communications in con-
> struction...contained specifications of
> the goals of work and prices; they did not
> contain the actual directives of work,
> which, it seemed to us, did not have to
> be there because they were already incor-
> porated in the professionalized culture of
> the workers. (1959, 181-182)

Studying the construction industry and trying to defend the rationality of its organizational form, Stinchcombe analyzed mass production only as a polar opposite of the conditions prevailing in the construction industry. His comparison is between the construction industry and the classic

---

*As Stinchcombe uses the term, professionalization "means that workers get technical socialization to achieve a publicly recognized occupational competence." (1959, 168) Under this criterion the only difference between professionalized occupations and others is the public recognition of the working knowledge required.

model of bureaucratized organization. If he had analyzed actual cases of mass production work organizations, he would have found his craft administration there too.

As Stinchcombe indicated, bureaucratic administration depends upon routinization of the work and the work product. When each product varies, routinization and therefore bureaucratic administration based on fixed rules and procedures is not possible (cf. Blauner, 1964, 35). Yet the product is not the only variable in the work situation.

Under conditions of mass production, it is possible that variability may persist in other aspects of the work environment. Where such variability persists, that aspect of the work environment becomes a subject area of supplementary working knowledge. In the Cone Department, there remain significant areas of variability in the materials processed and in the operation of the machinery. The bank is much more highly bureaucratized, yet even there, aspects of the work situation are not routinized -- notably the work role behavior of other tellers in the preparation of reports. In fact, Mr. Davis turned around the productivity and morale situation at the bank primarily by following the strategy of recognizing the tellers' working knowledge (thus "professionalizing" it by extending it recognition and legitimacy in the organization) and by encouraging the tellers to use this knowledge for the "craft administration" of their daily report preparation.

Total routinization of the work situation would require the transformation of all variable aspects of that situation into constants. Such total routinization is not possible. At a bare minimum, the role behavior of customers or of other workers in the environment remains resolutely variable, as the human relations school of Industrial Sociology emphasized.

Nevertheless, it is true that in processes of mass production, more aspects of the work environment are routinized into constants than is true in craft industries that produce single units. The working knowledge acquired is therefore less than is the case with craftsmen in traditional trades. This is the heart of Braverman's (1975) analysis of the "degradation of work in the twentieth century."* Yet craft administration of production persists,

---

*The quoted phrase is the book's subtitle.

despite the decline of the craft knowledge possessed by individual workers.

This combination of declining individual working knowledge and persisting craft administration points to a development in the method of craft decision-making that is lost in both Stinchcombe's and Braverman's analyses. In traditional trades, the "culture" that craftsmen use to guide their work is collective, but craft administration decisions are made by individuals. In mass production situations, the craft administration decisions are more collective. They have to be, both because the complex division of labor makes the work more interdependent and because individual workers no longer possess the all-around stock of working knowledge necessary to make decisions affecting others in the work situation as well as themselves.

The craft administration in mass production work situations therefore necessarily takes on a more collective and cooperative character. Such decisions can only be made by groups of workers holding different jobs, but linked by their communal network. This collective, cooperative kind of craft administration is not an indicator of the "degradation of work." To the contrary -- and Marxists like Braverman should be able to see this -- it reflects the essential Marxist vision of the revolutionary proletariat as the carriers of the ideals of socialism. Their everyday work experience teaches them to cooperate, overcomes petty bourgeois individualism, joins them in solidarity, and trains them in the democratic, collective administration of large-scale, technologically sophisticated production organizations.*

Conflict Between Workers' Craft Administration and Management's Bureaucratic Administration

Management must depend upon working knowledge of workers to effectively deal with remaining areas of variation. Management may recognize this explicit-

---

*Although as a former printer I share Braverman's nostalgia for the craftsman's life (He is a former coppersmith.), it is a serious mistake to think we represented a more revolutionary force than workers in blue and white collar mass production jobs. In fact, as Lenin (1917, 775) emphasized, our individualistic work conditions were the sources of our petty bourgeois predilections for social democracy and trade union econoimism.

169

ly, as Mr. Davis appears to do in the bank, it may
"recognize" it tacitly, as in the Cone Department,
by refraining from attempts to issue regulations requiring fixed procedures for the handling of variable processes, or it may attempt to issue such
regulations, in which case workers like the production control clerk, Roy's machine operators (1955),
or Valmeras' office workers (1971) must get the work
done by ignoring such regulations in their craft
administration decisions.

This research found many examples where management directives followed the type that according to
Stinchcombe are characteristic of craft administration situations -- the work goal is specified, often
with a deadline attached, but the procedures for
accomplishing the goal are left up to the workers
themselves. Notably, all of the training programs
observed operated on this basis. The worker doing
the training is expected to accomplish it within a
given time limit (three days in the Cone Department,
one week in the Bank), but the means of doing the
training are left totally unspecified. There were
also other circumstances where the work orders perhaps should follow such a form, since management
lacks specific knowledge of the detail variables
involved, but procedures are specified anyway. In
such cases, the procedures are ignored. For some
observers (Roy, 1955; Valmeras, 1971), this is
evidence of managerial irrationality, caused by the
desire to retain total control of the work. Yet
such management regulations are only irrational if
we assume that both workers and management have the
same goal, the effective accomplishment of concrete
work tasks. Such is not the case. Management has
the additional goals of maximizing profits (and,
to accomplish this, minimizing costs) and of maintaining organizational flexibility. Workers have
the additional goals of maintaining high standards
of quality, increasing convenience, and ensuring
the continued existence of their jobs. The conflict
between craft administration and bureaucratic administration occurs because of these conflicting goals.

Some examples of craft administration from the
case studies will illustrate how these differences
in work goals can affect craft administration decisions. In the past year the tellers have: reorganized the system of assigning and compiling
daily reports, established a filing system of pre-
printed forms to speed up the processing of the pay-
checks received by mail from their customers'
employers; and established the new rules governing

170

the exchange of money between tellers. As a result
of this exercise in collective planning and coordination -- that is, as a result of their own self-
management -- the tellers have eliminated important
sources of tension and conflict within the group and
greatly increased their working efficiency (thus
allowing them all to go home an hour earlier every
day). The material handlers in the Cone Department
figured out so many short-cut ways of getting their
work done that they created a problematic situation
for themselves in which management, seeing them
"standing around", would assign them what they considered unnecessary make-work. They also feared
that management would eventually realize the situation and lay off some material handlers. They resolved these problems by having the material handlers on each "side" work out a system of alternat-
ing illegitimate work breaks and by requiring that
the workers on these breaks leave the work floor so
they cannot be seen "standing around." This is also
an instance of worker self-management. In the bank,
efficiency-increasing work decisions were rewarded
with earlier departure times. In the factory,
management's anticipated response was unnecessary
work and possible layoffs. These two patterns of
management behavior were known to workers in both
situations, and this knowledge was an important
factor in determining the craft administration
decisions eventually worked out within the communal
network.

Craft administration decisions and bureaucratic
administration decisions come into conflict not only
because the goals that they pursue are different,
but also because management must retain ultimate
long-range control over the work. In the theory of
capitalist production, the decision-making functions
of planning and coordination must be carried out by
management, because the external conditions outside
of the firm -- the markets in which the firm buys
raw materials and labor, and sells its products --
are unstable and subject to rapidly changing conditions. To compete, the firm must remain flexible,
must be capable of rapid internal change to respond
to changing external conditions. In theory, only
management can make these decisions about how to
change the firm internally to adapt to changed
external conditions. This is because only management is in a position where it can constantly moni-
tor the external markets, and because only management does not have a vested interest in the firm's
current operations. The vested interests that

171

workers have, and management doesn't, are the workers' jobs. Management can decide "for the good of
the company" to phase out certain production lines,
eliminate departments, and even close whole plants,
without any conflict between the interests of stockholders and the interests of management. In such
cases, the interests of workers are in obvious conflict with those of the stockholders. This is the
reason why, in the theory of capitalist organization, the success and survival of the firm in the
market place requires the planning and coordinating
functions to be in the hands of management.

In four of the work situations studied, workers
reported recent management efforts to institute
major changes in the work. The four situations
illustrate differences in management's appraoch to
the problem, in workers' response, and in final out-
come. Comparison of these four situations is in-
structive, revealing the limits of both craft and
bureaucratic administration, of worker and managerial control.*

In the bank, the reorganization that was effected when Mr. Davis came to the branch a year ago is
acclaimed by everybody in the situation as a great
success. The efficiency and productivity of the
tellers has been increased. The number of settlement errors has been greatly reduced. Worker morale
is up: they can now do their owrk more efficiently,
with less tensions and problems, and leave an hour
earlier in the day.

> This is much better; the day doesn't seem
> so hectic and disorganized . . . . I go home
> in the afternoon, I don't feel like col-
> lapsing like I used to.

In this case, management made the change in the work
situation by promoting some of the workers and by
actively encouraging the others to get together and
figure out new procedures to solve some of their
problems. In other words, Mr. Davis encouraged the
development of craft administration, which had been
largely missing because the branch and its workers
were so new. It is noteworthy that this most

---

*Actually, the meatcutters were a fifth such case, but
they were interviewed so early in the study that the
importance of the issue had not become clear. The interviews therefore do not contain sufficient data for the case
to be included in this analysis.

172

successful example of a management-initiated change
in the work process is the one which did not involve
a managerial policy shift redefining the concrete
work tasks to be accomplished. In this case, management's only goal was to perform the old work
functions more effectively, a goal that was in this
case shared by the workers themselves. Also, the
changes in the work process were not initiated by
management directly, but were initiated by the workers themselves as a result of management's encouragement.

In the radiator shop, the previous management
attempted to impose changes in the work process,
and the workers resisted these changes. The result
was a classic confrontation, similar to the one
described by F. W. Taylor, the founder of "scientific management," in his testimony before a Congress-
ional hearing (1911), except that in this case the
workers "won". The previous management of the
radiator shop responded to the recession of 1969-70
by attempting to expand into new markets. The shop
had always made high quality, heavy duty truck
radiators. These were sold to owners of trucking
fleets, either as upgrading replacements for
standard radiators or as a part of the specifications made by these fleet owners when placing a
large order with truck manufacturers. Management
tried to increase its market share by switching its
sales efforts from fleet owners to truck manufacturers themselves. To successfully bid for this new
business, it was necessary to produce a lower priced
line of radiators than had previously been done.
Management attempted to do this by changing some
design elements, by specifying less expensive
materials, and by keeping the labor costs down.
This last goal was accomplished by setting lower
piece rates on these new radiators than the prevailing rates for comparable work on the old designs
and by actively pushing for an increase in productivity through traditional labor intensification
methods.

Workers found everything about this new policy
objectionable. They disliked both the lower quality
standards and the intensification of the work. They
responded with traditional job action methods --
slowdowns and wildcats -- and with a new technique
that proved effective. They called in OSHA (Occupational Safety and Health Administration) to complain
about the unsafe working conditions in the old shop.
The OSHA inspectors required the installation of a
shop-wide ventilation system. Management threatened

173

to close the shop and move south. Workers responded
by replacing their old Italian leaders in the union
local with a younger and tougher group made up
mostly of blacks with a few token Italian militants.

The whole situation was a disaster for management: it was losing money on each of the low cost
units that it put out, and many old customers were
switching over to these new lower cost models.
Finally, the company was sold to a larger conglomerate. The new conglomerate already made cheap
radiators in other plants and wanted to use this
plant in the way it had traditionally always been
used, for the small batch production of specialty
radiators for specialized or unusually heavy duty
applications. The new management cut back from a
two shift operation to one. Almost half the workers
were laid off, but for those who remained, the
battle was won.

In this case, management's reading of the changed external conditions was probably correct. The
company's radiator production was aimed at too small
a proportion of the overall truck-radiator market.*
The suggested policy change, however, was disas-
trous, because management assumed that the actual
administration of production was in its hands alone,
and that the implementation of policy decisions
would, therefore, pose no insurmountable problems.
This was wrong -- when the communal network in the
shop lost its fundamental ambivalence and switched
over from a craft administration stance to one of
total commitment to counterplanning, management
found it could not get its radiators produced at
acceptably cost-effective rates of productivity.

The third situation in which management tried to
implement new policies in response to changing
market conditions was a contract research office.
With the change to a Republican administration,
there were fewer and fewer contracts available for
the kind of ghetto community services that the
company had previously specialized in. Top management made the decision to go where the money is and
to move into the field of health care delivery,

---

*Under the new management, the operation is even smaller
than it previously was. This is probably acceptable in
its new role as a small part of a larger radiator-
producing operation. It was unacceptable in the context
of the previous company's operation, in which it was the
only radiator-manufacturing unit of a company that made
and marketed many different types of auto parts.

primarily in the study of the provision of care to
the institutionalized -- nursing homes and the like.
The office staff resisted this change in the concrete content and meaning of their jobs by sabotag-
ing the company's efforts to pursue contracts in
these new fields. Primarily, this was done by "for-
getting" to remind their superiors of relevant factors (deadlines, contract requirements) that had to
be taken into account for the company to bid
successfully on these new types of contracts, but
sometimes the sabotage took the more active form of
misaddressing envelopes, failing to meet typing
deadlines, etc.

Management finally handled this situation by
reorganizing their entire corporate structure,
creating five separate divisions, each with a
particular area of expertise. One of these divisions included the old community services work, and
the bulk of the black employees who were committed
to this type of work were shifted into this division. This division is headed by the black vice
president, whose presence at the presentation of
contract proposals to the various HEW agencies was
indispensable in the late '60's but is no longer so
necessary. In the two and a half years since this
division was formed, the number of its contracts
has been shrinking, and it has been forced to lay
off some of its overhead personnel. This strategy
of implementing policy changes by making an end run
around existing workers is the same as that observed
by Watson in his study of an auto plant. (Watson,
1971)

In the insurance company, management was con-
fronted with a situation where the mail carriers'
work community had gradually "displaced" the primary
work goal, delivering the mail, with another goal,
boosting the morale of the employees in the offices
that they visited. Mail delivery was sacrificed,
when necessary, in order to pursue various morale-
boosting activities, like the merchandising of
marijuana. Management's solution was to bring in a
new supervisor, who would be able to maintain
rapport with the mailmen while routinizing their
work and directly supervising their performance.
The new supervisor has confined his actions almost
exclusively to an effort to impose certain minimal
"constants" in the situation -- twice daily deliveries at scheduled times. In this case management has
been successful, if the goal was to improve mail
service. If the goal of upper management was to
eliminate illegal or illegitimate behavior, this

goal has not been successfully achieved. Indeed,
the new supervisor has not even attempted it.

The differences among these four examples of
management's efforts to take more control over the
work suggest some of the factors that shape the
course of managerial innovation efforts and workers'
response to them. In the bank and the mail department, where managements were most successful, managements' goals were more limited; the changes the
workers were asked to accommodate themselves to,
less drastic. In both cases, management was simply
reaffirming the work assignments and concrete work
goals that had always been present. In the radiator
shop and the contract research office, workers were
asked to accept new concrete work goals that funda-
mentally transformed the particular interpretations
of meaningfulness that they had created for their
work. In both cases, managements were totally
unsuccessful in forcing the workers involved to
accept the proposed redefinitions of the work. Yet
in these cases, the workers cannot be said to have
"won" either, since in each situation half of them
were eventually laid off.

In the bank and the mail room workers were persuaded to use their working knowledge to resume
craft administration of the work. In the bank, the
work and the workers were new. They were slowly
developing working knowledge and craft administration abilities anyway. Mr. Davis was a catalyst
whose explicit encouragement speeded up the process.
In the mail room, the clerks have come to accept the
new constant conditions. They now use their working
knowledge to make it possible to handle the increased work load while still maximizing the time and
effort available for their informal activities.

In the radiator shop and the contract research
office, workers withheld their craft administration
practices from management until management conceded
the impossibility of carrying on under these conditions, and permitted the workers to return to
their old work assignments. Yet in both cases,
management was able to salvage the situation (by
selling out to invest elsewhere, and by organizing
new divisions) so that they were able to pursue
their long-run goal of profit maximization, while
half the workers were unable to pursue their work
goals at all. These outcomes for workers and management accurately reflect the relative degrees of
control that each's mode of administration affords
them under present conditions in the development of
capitalism.

8. Working Knowledge: A Summary Statement

The purpose of this chapter is to pull together into one place the findings, generalizations and theoretical statements about working knowledge that have been presented discursively in the previous three chapters. Since this is a summary these findings are stated here flatly, almost in the form of propositions. Left out are the inductive or deductive logics that lie behind their formulation, the illustrations from this research and the references to the sociological work of others that illustrate and clarify the points, and some of the hedging and caveats that surround these points in the body of the text.

What is Working Knowledge?

In order to do their jobs successfully, all workers must acquire a stock of working knowledge. Every job requires the worker who holds it to act in the workplace, and to act effectively the worker must acquire a stock of working knowledge about that workplace. This working knowledge forms a holistic paradigm which each worker uses to structure her perception of the work environment and to interpret the various phenomena that occur within it.

Each stock of working knowledge may be broken down and analyzed by looking at the distinct phenomena in the work environment that becomes subject areas of working knowledge. In general, workers only learn about those phenomena in the work environment that affect their own work as they attempt to carry out their assigned jobs. To become a subject of working knowledge, therefore, phenomena in the work environment must present certain properties to the worker. Workers only learn about recurring variables, the variation of which they must take

177

into account in order to successfully perform their work tasks.

Examining the phenomena in the work environment that meet these requirements, it is possible to develop a classification scheme that divides any stock of working knowledge into five subject areas. Unless one of these types of phenomena is completely absent from the work environment, a worker's knowledge will include the following subject areas: basic working knowledge of routine procedures; and supplementary working knowledge about the materials (or documents) handled, the machinery used, expected patterns of customer or client behavior, and the expected work-role behavior of others in the work organization (including management) with whom the worker must interact in the performance of his job. Like any other such taxonomy, this classification scheme is useful because it permits the discovery and description of individual stocks of working knowledge more quickly yet more completely than would otherwise be possible.

Knowledge of routine procedures is called basic working knowledge because it is in constant use during the performance of work tasks and because it becomes so thoroughly assimilated that it can guide habitualized work activity without conscious effort on the part of the experienced worker. Supplementary working knowledge is used to overcome obstacles to routine work activities, to avoid potential disruptions, or to solve problems that interfere with productive work. Supplementary working knowledge is used only periodically and is applied consciously to permit the worker to continue or resume routine activity.

The amount of working knowledge necessary on a particular job is determined by the degree of specialization and routinization involved. Specialization refers to the number of work functions assigned to the job; routinization to the degree of variation in the performance of each function. Specialization results in a lessening of the basic working knowledge necessary; routinization a lessening of the supplementary working knowledge necessary. Since supplementary working knowledge, being consciously applied to overcome more difficult sorts of problems, is the more creative of the two types of knowledge, routinization is a more stultifying process than specialization. Fortunately, there are stricter technical limits on the degree of routinization that management can introduce. Extreme routinization is only possible under conditions of large scale mass processing of identical products from unvarying inputs.

An additional factor which influences how much knowledge a worker must learn on the job is the amount of overlap between the knowledge required by the job and the knowledge already possessed by ordinary members of the work force. The more esoteric the knowledge required by the job, the more the worker must learn, and the more likely it is that the importance of the working knowledge will be recognized, both by the workers themselves and by others. In some cases, therefore, while the process of specialization diminishes the overall amount of working knowledge necessary, it may nevertheless lead to an increased appreciation of the more esoteric knowledge that remains.

Since jobs that are generally considered "skilled" work are normally less routinized than most "unskilled" work, the popular division of jobs into "skilled" and "unskilled" categories bears some relation to the relative amounts of working knowledge necessary for each type of job. The problem with these labels is that the use of the "unskilled" label has led to a gross under-estimation of the amount of working knowledge actually necessary in these jobs. There is no such thing as unskilled work. The term demeans the workers involved, and it misleads all who seek to understand the nature of their work.

The Labor Department's use of the "semi-skilled" category to distinguish those who operate machines from those who do not is even more misleading. If anything, the operation of machinery may require less working knowledge, since these jobs are usually more specialized and more routinized than jobs involving ordinary manual labor alone.

A further advantage which the working knowledge concept offers over the concept of skill results from the traditional definition of "skill" as a combination of know-how and manual dexterity. The identification of skill (or the lack thereof) as a characteristic of manual work means that an attempt to apply the concept to the proliferating number of routinized white collar jobs leads only to increased confusion. Working knowledge is a more generalized concept, applying equally well to blue collar and white collar workers.

The conceptualization in terms of working knowledge therefore offers the following advantages over the traditional conceptualization in terms of skill: it substitutes a clear appreciation of the

179

necessary amount of working knowledge in every job
in place of the misleading belief that many jobs are
"unskilled"; its analytical breakdown of working
knowledge into constituent subject areas makes the
knowledge easier to identify and comparatively
evaluate;* its analysis of the effects of routinization and specialization pinpoints the organizational
determinant of the amount of working knowledge
necessary in various jobs; and it is a more inclusive concept, equally useful in the study of either
blue collar or white collar jobs.

Once working knowledge has been understood as a
phenomenon in itself -- once its content and its
organizational determinants have been clarified --
it is possible to examine its effects in the work
place. This is important because a better grasp of
the importance of working knowledge in jobs that
are normally considered "unskilled" leads to improved understanding of many of the issues that have
dominated the study of workers and work organizations.

Working Knowledge and Alienation

Traditional discussions of alienation have
tended toward oversimplification because of a fail-
ure to fully recognize the effect of working knowledge on alienation. If alienation is accepted as a
concept having both objective and subjective aspects,
then it can be said that, through their learning of
working knowledge, workers are able to counteract to
some degree the alienating aspects of their work
situations. This is at least partly a conscious
strategy. In discussing why they learn working
knowledge, workers give reasons that can be readily
interpreted as attempts to reduce powerlessness or
to render the work more meaningful. The learning of
working knowledge is one of two major strategies,
the other being participation in the work community,
that workers use in their efforts to overcome alienation. Working knowledge ameliorates both the subjective and objective aspects of all four of Blauner's usages of the concept -- powerlessness, meaninglessness, self-estrangement, and social isolation.

---

*As an additional side benefit, it is also easier to pene-
trate the mystique that some occupational groups have tried
to create around the esoteric knowledge of their (usually
"professional") jobs.

Powerlessness. Each subject area of supplementary working knowledge -- the materials, the
machines, the customers, the management and the
other workers -- represents an aspect of the physical or social environment that workers are better
able to manipulate and control as a result of what
they have learned.

Meaninglessness. Working knowledge also inter-
prets events in the work environment, rendering
them meaningful by explaining or accounting for them
in the context of the paradigmatic overview of the
work situation that working knowledge provides. By
the same token, working knowledge provides workers
with a meaningful interpretation of their own work
activity. Despite all the nonsense that has been
written to the contrary, workers do in fact know
the effect of their work on: the overall work
process, other workers further along the work flow,
the realization of the goals of the work organization, and the members of the general public who
consume the goods or services that the workers produce.
     True, the interpretation of meaning that the
working knowledge provides often does result in the
phenomenon of "goal displacement." That is, work
goals that policy makers in the organization consider to be only subsidiary means towards some larger end become for the workers involved ends in themselves. However, it must be pointed out that at
least in capitalist work organizations, where the
ultimate goal is the pursuit of profit and the intermediate goals are the production of useful (and
therefore marketable) goods and services, then the
workers' goal displacement (that is, their concentration on the concrete production of useful goods
and services) is more likely to better serve society
than management's pursuit of the organizational
goal of profit.

Self-estrangement. In so far as working knowledge provides work activity with intrinsic meaning
to supplement the extrinsic meaning it already has
for the worker as a means to earn a living, then
working knowledge helps to overcome self-estrangement. Yet for most jobs and occupations, self-
estrangement is the aspect of alienation that working knowledge is least effective in overcoming.
This is because the working knowledge that provides

181

the intrinsic meaningfulness is not shared outside the work community. Worse than that -- society does not even acknowledge that such working knowledge exists (except in the case of jobs in management, the professions, and a dwindling number of traditional skilled trades). Thus, although working knowledge can lessen self-estrangement by defining the work within the work community as intrinsically meaningful, self-estrangement will persist as long as the working knowledge and the intrinsic meaning it provides are not recognized by others, especially management on the job and family and friends off the job.

Social Isolation. Working knowledge helps to overcome social isolation by providing one of the necessary bases for the formation of work communities. Since working knowledge is determined by the structure of the work environment, shared work environments lead to shared working knowledge. Since such shared knowledge is one of the prerequisites for the formation of work communities, then working knowledge helps to overcome social isolation by contributing to the formation of these communal relationships.

Workers also combat their own alienation through formation of a work community. Work communities are multi-faceted "informal" relations among workers who share at least certain aspects of their work environment and therefore of their working knowledge, who are forced in the course of their work to engage in face to face interaction, and whose successful work performance depends on each other's mutual cooperation. Work communities are not closed-bounded groups: at least in large and complex work organizations, it is more appropriate to think of them as a network of communal relations that extends throughout the whole organization.

Participation in the work community is a technical requirement of production, instrumentally necessary to build up relations of trust and cooperation among people whose work assignments require their frequent interaction. Nevertheless, these instrumental Gesellschaft relations, originally entered into only because their jobs require them, are transformed into holistic Gemeinschaft relations, valued in themselves and carried on for their own sake.

Participation in work communities also tends to reduce all facets of alienation, most obviously social isolation, but also self-estrangement, mean-

182

inglessness and powerlessness. Self-estrangement is reduced because participation in the work community transforms the job from a mere means of earning a living (that is, of sustaining a "real" life off the job) into a life activity of its own. Meaninglessness is reduced because the tasks and requirements of the job are transformed into communal obligations, as doing one's "fair share" becomes a community norm. Powerlessness is reduced through participation in the planning and counterplanning of the work that occurs within the work community.*

Though the learning of working knowledge and the participation in communal networks may reduce alienation, they cannot eliminate it altogether. The workers' interviews reveal an attitude toward their work that can only be described as one of fundamental ambivalence. Mutually contradictory elements of commitment and alienation coexist uneasily in their consciousness. This ambivalence accurately reflects the reality of their work situations, where the working knowledge and communal relationships that reduce alienation are fragile social constructions, dependent for their existence on conditions in the work environment over which management retains ultimate control.

Working Knowledge and Work Control

Just as the analysis of working knowledge and the functions of communal networks sheds new light on previous discussions of alienation, it also illuminates traditional discussions of authority and control over the work process. Using their working knowledge and working through their communal networks, workers administer routine work processes, to an extent not usually understood in the literature of industrial sociology. They do this not as a result of any victorious struggles for "workers' control" but because only they possess the specific knowledge necessary for the detailed planning and coordination that are necessary to administer routine production. The "craft administration of production" is not replaced in complex organizations by "bureaucratic administration" but maintains an unacknowledged existence in the day-to-day administration of production.

_____

*See the discussion below of the relationship between working knowledge and work control.

183

The craft administration of production is an
expression on the part of workers of their non-
alienated commitment to the work. It is also
absolutely necessary for organizational productivity, as "work to rule" job actions repeatedly demonstrate. Some observers have noted therefore the
apparent irrationality of management's attempts to
suppress craft administration.

Although craft administration generally contributes to the organization, it does pose two
genuine problems for management. First, there are
the obvious differences in work goals between management and the workers. Craft administration
emphasizes quality production and work convenience
at the expense of production speed, production quantity, and profit maximization through cost minimi-
zation. There is also a second less frequently
noticed problem that the craft administration of
production causes for management. Organizational
success over time depends not only on extracting
high rates of profit from current production activities, but also on maintaining organizational flexibility to meet changing conditions outside the
organization. Companies do go bankrupt, even very
large ones, and when they do it is usually because
they have been unable to adapt themselves to changes
in markets or government regulations that affect the
company.

As management sees it, organizational flexibility depends on what it sometimes called its "manageability." In this context, manageability refers
simply to the extent of total management control.
Manageable organizations are those in which organizational innovations can be initiated from the top
through a simple process of command. Unmanageable
organizations are ones in which such commands either
do not effect change or effect such change only
after a long process of conflict. The more craft
administration carried on by workers, the more unmanageable the organization for management.

Workers' resistance to such management initiatives is not due to some "traditional orientation"
on the part of these workers that resists all
change. As new working knowledge is acquired and
the organizational skills of the work community
develop, workers frequently initiate innovations of
their own, some of which are opposed by management,
and not because of management's "traditional orientation," either. Workers resist managerial innovations when such innovations further the particular

184

goals of management at the expense of the particular goals of workers, or when such innovations threaten to disrupt the working knowledge and the work communities that workers have developed.

This last point expresses the core of the relationship between working knowledge and control over the work process. Working knowledge increases workers' control over their work environments, yet working knowledge is itself ultimately dependent upon those same work environments. Through organizational innovation, management may transform these environments. This has the effect, whether intended or accidental, of disrupting working knowledge and communal networks. The control over the work process that workers acquire through their working knowledge and participation in craft administration may be reduced at any time by management decisions that "shake up" the organization and transform the work enviornments within it.

Therefore, although workers do "control" their own workplaces and their own day-to-day actions more than has been previously noticed, the control they exercise is not legitimized or institutionalized, even where workers are represented by unions. To note that working knowledge is a source of worker's control is to raise the possibility and plausibility of institutionalizing that control, of creating real worker self-management, but it is not to suggest that workers' emancipation has already somehow secretly occurred. Workers and their advocates will not wake tomorrow to find that the revolution is already made, but they may wake to discover that the revolutionary society is less distant -- less impossibly utopian -- than it yesterday appeared.

9. Some Implications:
A Final Note

Each interview in this research project would
typically begin with the worker telling me something
like this machine operator's comment:

> I don't know why you want to interview
> me. You don't have to know anything to
> do my job.

Three hours later, too exhausted to keep writing
down all she knew, I brought the interview to a
close. As I was preparing to leave, she told me
something entirely different, and this too was
typical.

> This was real interesting. You don't get a
> chance to stop and think about things like
> this, usually. Lily* was right: it wasn't
> embarrassing or anything; it was more
> enjoyable, like. . . . It really makes you
> think, all the things we do that we don't
> even realize.

No, we don't even realize -- not social scientists, not managers, and most regrettably, not even
workers themselves -- the amount of know-how necessary on every job, the amount of judgement that
workers must use, the amount of effective responsibility they must routinely exercise. Despite generations of managerial efforts to centralize
decision-making in its own hands, to replace workers' judgements with machine programs, the American
economy still firmly depends on the know-how of

---

*The previously interviewed worker who had helped set up this
interview, following the snowball sampling procedure.

workers, and on their willingness to use that know-
how to guide their collective work.

Workers themselves fail to recognize the valuable extent of their own contributions to social
production. Workers themselves believe that they
really are just an easily replaceable piece of the
organization their employers manage, just like an
interchangeable part of the machines the workers
themselves operate. This is the essential human
tragedy of our economy, the "hidden injury" that
afflicts American workers as a class. (Sennett and
Cobb, 1972)

I find it ironic that the highly influential,
award winning study of the recent history of the
American work process, Braverman's Labor and Monopoly Capital, should so heavily reinforce the
general misconception that work has become completely "degraded," workers completely "deskilled."
Ironic because Braverman, a life-long Marxist despite having spent the last twenty years of his life
in publishing management, arrived at his conclusions
not by studying the activities of actual workers
nor even by studying the activities of actual managers, but by studying managerial writings about the
increasing control they hoped to acquire over workplaces by removing decision making authority from
workers. Not for the first time, a Marxist has
attributed all active power to management, reducing
workers to the role of helpless victims of their
own increasing immiseration.

Trying perhaps to strengthen his critique of
contemporary capitalism, he accepts too uncritically
the most nightmarish proposals of managerial
theorists as having in fact been accomplished. In
particular, Braverman believed that:

> Taylorism dominates the world of produc-
> tion. . . . If Taylorism does not exist
> as a separate school today, it is because,
> apart from the bad odor of the name, it is
> no longer the property of a faction, since
> its fundamental teachings have become the
> bedrock of all work design. (1974, 87)

Even though descriptive generalizations based
on this research must be extremely tentative since
the number of workplaces studied is so small, I now
believe that Braverman was wrong about the wide-
spread application of Taylorism. Even in the few
workplaces where there can be found industrial
engineers and time study men -- those descendents of

Taylor -- management ignores Taylor's "task idea," which Taylor himself thought was central to his enterprise. (1911, 1967) Workers are still left to their own devices, and the "rule of thumb method" that Taylor so despised is still as prevalent as ever, because management never bothers to break a job down into its minute component tasks, let alone to figure out the "one best way" to do such tasks. Taylor's "scientific management" was mostly an ideology, an ideal many managers aspired to and experimented with, perhaps, but one never put into substantial practice. It did profoundly influence industrial engineers and production designers, as Braverman said, but once given the organization of the work flow and the design of the equipment, workers are pretty much left alone to figure out how to make it work.

The only present day Taylorists that I've heard of are the managers at the United Parcel Service and, possibly, at the United States Postal Service. Why? I don't know, but it is interesting that the insurance company mail clerk I interviewed had also experienced something Taylor-like. But the system there was specifically instituted to insure managerial control, to force the mail clerks to take longer at their jobs so they would have less time to make book, market drugs, and jive with the women. The management's new sort-first-then-deliver system was less efficient, and tacitly acknowledged as such by the manager involved.

The point of these remarks is not to belabor Braverman. His is a brilliant work, fully deserving of its C. Wright Mills Award. Like Blauner's work of a decade earlier, and in fact like many of the basic works of the great "classical" sociologists, Labor and Monopoly Capital has the great virtue of stimulating the "sociological imagination" (Mills, 1959) of its readers, contributing hugely to the advance of social science even though major portions of its arguments may turn out to be substantially incorrect.

Braverman's failings are significant precisely because they are not the idiosyncratic errors of one individual. They represent widespread deficiencies in contemporary Marxist social science, deficiencies that have lamentable consequences for Marxist analyses of important areas of current social policy debate.

Basic to any methodology of Marxist social science is a conception of the necessary relation of "theory and practice." Commonly, this has been

taken to mean a kind of left pragmatism. Working
in alliance with a social movement of some sort,
Marxist intellectuals analyze social reality, the
movement formulates its strategy on the basis of
this analysis, and the validity of the analysis
is confirmed or disconfirmed by the relative success
of the movement in achieving its particular goals of
social change. Even the most abstract Marxist
theorizing is supposed to be in essence an applied
social science, a "policy science," if you like, of
the left.

As a general methodology, this is fine -- in
periods of popular insurgency, when there are
genuinely mass-based social movements to discipline
the social scientists, urgently demanding and constantly testing the applicability of the scientists'
analyses. In the intervening period between waves
of mass movement, however, the methodology is un-
workable. Those who nevertheless try to apply it
end up too often as intellectualizing apologists for
the most ludicrous "line" of little sectarian group-
lets. Most American Marxist social scientists, fortunately, choose "independence" over sectarianism
in these periods of relative quiescence. But this
independence has its own danger: the social scientist's analysis loses its anchor in the actual
experiences of the mass movement and its members.

Adrift in the abstract world of academic dis-
course, the Marxist's analysis too easily falls into a distorted view of reality because it is now
detached from its only verification principle,
political practice. Thus for example Braverman and
Braverman's academic audience, because they lack any
institutionalized means through which workers can
tell them they are wrong, can accept managers'
Taylorist fantasies as adequate representations of
workplace reality.

Because of what this research project taught me
about methodology, I would like to propose here an
alternative anchor, an interim verification
principle for Marxist social science in periods
between waves of popular insurgency. I make this
proposal with some strong feelings of trepidation,
because I don't believe it an adequate substitute
for the ultimate test of political practice, but I
do believe it is preferable to the two tacit verification principles that presently dominate Marxist
writing in social science: direct dependence on
resonating with the domain assumptions of the
Marxist social scientist and his academic Marxist
audience (Cf. Gouldner, 1970, 20-60): or reference

to the canonical texts. A better method of anchor-
ing Marxist theory would be a less inductivist, left
variant of Glaser and Strauss' method for the discovery of "grounded theory." (1969)
   A Marxist methodology for the grounding of
theoretical analysis differs substantially from
Glaser and Strauss' approach because it is based on
a wide Marxist perspective, a macro-historical viewpoint that serves as a paradigm base for Marxist
social research in the same Kuhnian way that rela-
tivity serves as a background paradigm for all contemporary work in physics. In their rhetoric,
Glaser and Strauss are pure inductivists, advocating that the researcher should enter the research
project with a tabula rasa mind, ready for whatever
insights the research experience will provide. This
is obvious nonsense. In their own research, they
work out of a basically symbolic interactionist
paradigm, properly impressed by their research subjects' ability to define their own situations, but
unable to distinguish which aspects of whose reality
definitions are most significant for the determination of the collective futures of us all.
   On the other hand, a Marxist methodology for
the development of grounded theory will differ from
present approaches to Marxist analysis because it
takes seriously Marx's maxim that social existence
determines social consciousness. Therefore, Marxist
analyses of any particular aspect of social reality
should be grounded in the consciousnesses of the
people who actually experience that reality.
Analyses of the work process must be grounded in the
experiences of working people.
   I am not advocating here that the researchers
uncritically accept everything their informants tell
them. The goal of Marxist social science is still
to unveil the present appearance of social phenomena,
to reveal the underlying essential social relations.
I am advocating, though, that researchers begin
their analyses by attempting to discover the insights and understandings of their informants. The
next step is to sort through these insights, re-
arranging them according to the researchers' own
more analytic and more inclusive paradigm. The
next and most important step in this verification
process is to return the analysis to the informants.
The analysis can be considered to be "grounded"
or tentatively verified if the informants' response
is something like: "Aha! Why didn't we think of
that? Now I see why so-and-so did such-and-such,
etc." This gratifying "aha" response, as I call it,

191

is the signal to the researchers that they have suc-
ceeded in putting into words, assembling into an
analytic framework, the less articulate perceptions
of the people whose social relations and social
experiences the researchers are trying to compre-
hend.

Following a methodology based on this principle
of verification-in-dialogue, Marxist social scientists can conduct research that imitates in the research process the political praxis of revolutionary
leaders who follow Mao's "mass line" approach or of
movement strategists who adopt the role of Gramsci's
"revolutionary intellectuals" in the struggle. As
pale an imitation of political praxis as this research strategy may be, it is nevertheless better
than research strategies which attempt no such
imitation whatsoever.

Because Marxist social science for so long now
has not been verified in the United States either by
mass movements of workers or by workers' participation in the research process, and also because
Marxist intellectuals have leaned so heavily on the
"false consciousness" thesis to explain why workers
find Marxist's studies of work irrelevant or un-
intelligible, Marxist writings about the work process have persisted in a fundamental error, one that
has important consequences for political strategies
and policy choices.

Overenamored of Marx's immiseration thesis
(that the lot of the worker under capitalism, "be
his payment high or low," gets worse and worse),
Marxists selectively perceive only the ugliness of
the labor process. This one-sided -- one might even
say non-dialectical -- view of the nature of work in
late capitalism has led to a tendency to forget that
even in the full flower of capitalist development,
work is still a unity of concrete and abstract
labor, of use value and exchange value production,
of real public utility and merely private profit.
These former aspects continue to provide workers
with some of the satisfaction and self-respect that
comes from learning, growing, and making a useful
contribution to society in the labor process.

If work was truly as degraded, workers truly as
de-skilled, as Braverman depicted, if a small per-
centage of technocratic managers truly had that
total a control over the production process, then
democratic socialism -- as opposed to the bureaucratic technocratic kind -- would become a utopian
fantasy, without basis in the developing mode of
production.

Yet work is a duality of both constructive and destructive, humanity-affirming and humanity-denying, aspects. Because this is so, worker's involvement with the specific skills and processes of their concrete labor is as "true" -- as in tune with the objective realities of capitalist production -- as their alienation. In fact, the struggle to remain involved, to combat alienation, is more than just an individual struggle for survival. It is an essential part of the class struggle. Day in and day out, exercising and realizing its capacities, the working class authentically upholds the value of productive labor and the dignity of productive laborers. Without the experience of this daily struggle against alienation, a working class revolution appears implausible, a socialist reconstruction impossible.

Most Marxists today, if they can perceive the job involvement of workers at all, consider it a part of false consciousness, an ideology to be overcome in the class struggle. I consider it a necessary element in that struggle: a constant touchstone against which every worker can test the specific capitalist relations she experiences and find them wanting; and an enduring foundation upon which, come the time, socialism must ultimately be built.

People who try to take pride and pleasure in their work are not merely false conscious fools, they are also the vanguard of a new socialist society, trapped in the sticky web of old capitalist production relations. Trying to do their job as they see it, they are recurrently getting clobbered upside the head with the message that, to their employers, the utility and quality of their product, even the efficiency and expertise of their work, are not as important as the pursuit of profit. The production goals of workers and the production goals of society are not the goals of capital, but only a means to the goal of endless self-enhancement.

This is the area where Marxist social science is most needed: to listen to and articulate this ambivalence of workers, to raise the issue explicitly in the popular culture, to provide the frame of reference that helps workers make sense out of this kind of experience. Workers knew about their own personal troubles with inflation, unemployment, race and sex discrimination, of course, but Marxist intellectuals helped make these topics into public issues. They have become staples of the nation's

193

understanding of its "social problems." Marxists
need do the same for the work experience, in both
its soul-enhancing and soul-destroying aspects. For
a movement against alienation and exploitation can
only come from strong people, as aware of their own
capabilities as they are of the debilitating power
of the institutions they seek to overthrow.

Bibliography

Baritz, Loren. 1960. The Servants of Power. Middleton, Conn.: Wesleyan University Press.

Bendix, Reinhard. 1956. Work and Authority in Industry. New York: John Wiley & Sons.

Bensmen, Joseph; and Gerver, Israel. 1964. "Crime and Punishment in the Factory: The Function of Deviancy in Maintaining the Social System," Social Forces. Vol. 42, n. 3.

Berger, Peter; Berger, Brigitte; and Kellner, Hans. 1974. The Homeless Mind. New York: Vintage.

Berger, Peter; and Luckmann, Thomas. 1970. The Social Construction of Reality. Garden City, New York: Doubleday-Anchor.

Blau, Peter M. 1955. The Dynamics of Bureaucracy. Chicago: University of Chicago Press.

Blauner, Robert. 1964. Alienation and Freedom:The Factory Worker and His Industry. Chicago: University of Chicago Press.

Blumberg, Paul. 1969. Industrial Democracy: The Sociology of Participation. New York: Schocken.

Braverman, Harry. 1974. Labor and Monopoly Capital. New York: Monthly Review Press.

Bright, J. R. 1971. "Does Automation Raise Skill Requirements?" Harvard Business Review. V. 36, n. 4, pp. 85-98.

Chinoy, Eli. 1955. Automobile Workers and the American Dream. Garden City, N. Y.: Doubleday.

Comte, Auguste. 1975. The Essential Writings, Ed. by Gertrude Lenzer. New York: Harper & Row.

Crozier, Michael. 1964. The Bureaucratic Phenomenon. Chicago: University of Chicago.

Crozier, Michael. 1973. The World of the Office Worker. New York: Schocken.

Davis, Fred. 1959. "The Cabdriver and His Fare: Facets of a Fleeting Relationship," American Journal of Sociology, 65, pp. 158-165.

Denzin, Norman K. 1970. The Research Act. Chicago: Aldine.

Dissent. 1972 (winter). "Special Issue: The World of the Blue Collar Worker."

Durkheim, Emile. 1950 (original 1895). The Rules of the Sociological Method. New York: Free Press.

Edwards, Richard C. 1975. "The Social Relations of Production in the Firm and Labor Market Structure," Politics and Society. V. 5, n. 1, pp. 88-108.

197

Faunce, William A. 1965. "Automation and the
    Division of Labor," Social Problems, V. 13, n.
    2, pp. 149-160.
Friedmann, Georges. 1955. Industrial Society. New
    York: Free Press.
Friedmann, Georges. 1964. The Anatomy of Work.
    New York: Free Press.
Glaser, Barney G., and Strauss, Anselm. 1967. The
    Discovery of Grounded Theory. Chicago:
    Aldine.
Gold, Raymond. 1958 (March). "Roles in Sociologi-
    cal Field Observations," Social Forces. 36.
Gordon, David M., Edwards, Richard D., and Reich,
    Michael. 1975. Labor Market Segmentation in
    American Capitalism. Lexington, Mass.: D. C.
    Heath.
Gorz, Andre. 1968. Strategy for Labor. Boston:
    Beacon Press.
Gorz, Andre. 1972. "Technical Intelligence and the
    Capitalist Division of Labor," Telos. Number
    12, pp. 27-41.
Gorz, Andre. 1973. Socialism and Revolution.
    Garden City, N.Y.: Doubleday-Anchor.
Gouldner, Alvin W. 1954. Patterns of Industrial
    Bureaucracy. New York: Free Press.
Gouldner, Alvin W. 1965. Wildcat Strike. New
    York: Harper.
Gouldner, Alvin W. 1970. The Coming Crisis of
    Western Sociology. New York: Basic.
Gramsci, Antonio. 1959. The Modern Prince and
    Other Writings. New York: International.
Grusky, Oscar, and Miller, George A., eds. 1970.
    The Sociology of Organizations: Basic Studies.
    New York: Free Press.
Habenstein, Robert W. 1970. Pathways to Data.
    Chicago: Aldine.
Hanson, Norwood R. 1958. Patterns of Discovery.
    New York: Cambridge University Press.
Holzner, Burkart. 1972. Reality Construction in
    Society, Rev. Ed. Boston: Schenkman.
Hughes, Everett C. 1958. Men and Their Work.
    Glencoe, Ill.: Free Press.
Israel, Joachim. 1971. Alienation: From Marx to
    Modern Sociology. Boston: Allyn & Bacon.
Jenkins, David. 1973. Job Power: Blue and White
    Collar Democracy. Garden City, N. Y.: Double-
    day.
Kolaja, Jiri. 1960. A Polish Factory. Lexington,
    Ky.: University of Kentucky.

198

Kuhn, Thomas S. 1970a. The Structure of Scientific Revolutions, 2nd Ed., Enlarged. Chicago: University of Chicago Press.

Kuhn, Thomas S. 1970b. "Reflection on my Critics" in Imre Lakatos and Alan Musgrave, eds., Criticism and the Growth of Knowledge. Cambridge University Press.

Kuhn, Thomas S. 1971. "Second Thoughts on Paradigms" in Frederick Suppe, Ed., The Structure of Scientific Theories. Urbana, Ill.: University of Illinois Press.

Lakatos, Imre, and Musgrave, Alan, eds. 1970. Criticism and the Growth of Knowledge. Cambridge: Cambridge University Press.

Landsberger, Henry A. 1958. Hawthorne Revisited. Ithaca, New York: Cornell University.

Lasson, Kenneth. 1971. The Workers. New York: Bantam.

Lupton, Thomas. 1963. On the Shop Floor: Two Studies of Workshop Organization and Output. New York: MacMillan.

Marcson, Simon, ed. 1970. Automation, Alienation and Anomie. New York: Harper & Row.

Marglin, Steve. 1974. "What Do Bosses Do?", Review of Radical Political Economy. V. 6, n. 2.

Marx, Karl. 1933 (original, 1849). Wage Labor and Capital. New York: International.

Marx, Karl. 1964 (original, 1847). The German Ideology. New York: International.

Marx, Karl. 1967 (original, 1867). Capital, Vol. I. New York: International.

Marx, Karl. 1969 (original, 1844). Economic and Philosophic Manuscripts of 1844. New York: International.

Marx, Karl. 1973 (original, 1857-58). Grundrisse. New York: Vintage.

Maslow, Abraham. 1954. Motivation and Personality. New York: Harper.

Masterman, Margaret. 1970. "The Nature of Paradigms," in Imre Lakatos and Alan Musgrave, Eds. Criticism and the Growth of Knowledge. Cambridge: Cambridge University Press.

Mathewson, Stanley B. 1931. Restriction of Output Among Unorganized Workers. New York: Viking.

Mechanic, David. 1972. "Sources of Power of Lower Participants in Complex Organizations", Administrative Science Quarterly, pp. 349-364.

Melman, Seymour. 1965. Our Depleted Society. New York: Holt, Rinehart, & Winston.

Mennerick, Lewis A. 1974. "Client Typologies," Sociology of Work and Occupations. Vol. 1, n. 4, pp. 396-418.

Merton, Robert K. 1968. Social Theory and Social Structure. Enlarged Edition. New York: Free Press.

Meszaros, Istvan. 1972. Marx's Theory of Alienaation. New York: Harper.

Miller, Delbert, and Form, William. 1964. Industrial Sociology. New York: Harper.

Mills, C. Wright. 1951. White Collar. New York: Oxford University Press.

Mills, C. Wright. 1959. The Sociological Imagination. New York: Oxford University Press.

Ollman, Bertell. 1971. Alienation: Marx's Conception of Man in Capitalist Society. New York: Cambridge University Press.

Peirce, C. S. S. 1955. Philosophical Writings of Peirce. Justus Buchler, ed. New York: Dover.

Ritzer, George. 1972. Man and His Work: Conflict and Change. New York: Appleton-Century-Crofts.

Robinson, John P., Athanasiou, Robert, and Head, Kendra B. 1969. Measures of Occupational Attitudes and Occupational Characteristics. Ann Arbor, Mich.: Survey Research Center, Institute for Social Research.

Rosow, Jerome. 1974. The Worker and the Job: Coping with Change. Englewood Cliffs, N. J.: Prentice-Hall.

Roy, Donald. 1952. "Quota Restriction and Goldbricking in a Machine Shop," American Journal of Sociology. V. 51, n. 5, pp. 427-442.

Roy, Donald. 1955. "Efficiency and 'the Fix', Informal Group Relations in a Piece Work Machine Shop," American Journal of Sociology. V. 60, pp. 255-266. Reprinted as "Making Out: A Counter-System of Workers' Control of Work Situation and Relationships," in Tom Burns, ed. Industrial Man, pp. 359-379. Baltimore: Penguin.

Roy, Donald F. 1960. "Banana Time: Job Satisfaction and Informal Interaction," Human Organization. N. 18, pp. 158-168.

Roy, Donald F. 1970. "Southern Labor Union Organizing Campaigns," in Robert W. Habenstein, Pathways to Data. Chicago: Aldine.

Rush, Harold, ed. 1969. Behavioral Science: Concepts and Management Applications. New York: The Conference Board.

Sayles, Leonard R. 1958. Behavior of Industrial Work Groups. New York: John Wiley & Sons.

Schacht, Richard. 1970. Alienation. Garden City, N.Y.: Doubleday-Anchor.

Schneider, Eugene. 1969. Industrial Sociology, 2nd Ed. New York: McGraw-Hill.

Schutz, Alfred. 1962. Collected Papers. Vol. I. The Hague: Nijhoff.

Schutz, Alfred. 1964. Collected Papers. Vol. II. The Hague: Nijhoff.

Seashore, Stanley. 1955. Group Cohesiveness in the Industrial Work Group. Ann Arbor, Mich.: Institute for Social Relations, University of Michigan Press.

Seeman, Melvin. 1959. "On the Meaning of Alienation," American Sociological Review. V. 24, n. 6, pp. 783-91.

Sennett, Richard, and Cobb, Jonathan. 1972. The Hidden Injuries of Class. New York: Random House.

Sexton, Patricia Cayo, and Sexton, Brendan. 1971 Blue Collars and Hard Hats. New York: Random House.

Shorter, Edward, ed. 1973. Work and Community in the West. New York: Harper & Row.

Shostak, Arthur B. 1969. Blue-Collar Life. New York: Random House.

Simmel, Georg. 1950. The Sociology of Georg Simmel, Ed. and trans. by Kurt H. Wolff. New York: Free Press.

Slater, Philip. 1970. The Pursuit of Loneliness. Boston: Beacon Press.

Smith, Adam. 1937 (original, 1776). The Wealth of Nations. New York: Modern Library.

Stinchcombe, Arthur L. 1959. "Bureaucratic and Craft Administration of Production," Administrative Science Quarterly. V. 4, pp. 168-187.

Stone, Kathy. 1974. "The Origins of Job Structures in the Steel Industry," Review of Radical Political Economy. V. 6, n. 2.

Swados, Harry. 1958. On the Line. Boston: Little, Brown.

Taylor, Frederick W. 1911. Scientific Management. New York: Harper Brothers.

Taylor, F. W. 1967 (original, 1911). The Principles of Scientific Management. New York: Norton.

Terkel, Studs. 1974. Working. New York: Pantheon.

Toennies, Ferdinand. 1957 (original, 1887). Com-
    munity and Society. East Lansing, Mich.:
    Michigan State University Press.
U. S., Special Task Force to the Secretary of Health,
    Education and Welfare. 1972. Work in America.
    Cambridge: MIT Press.
Valmeras, L. 1971. "The Work Community," Radical
    America. V. 5, n. 4, pp. 77-92.
Vanek, Jaroslav, ed. 1975. Self-Management.
    Baltimore: Penguin.
Veblen, Thorstein. 1914. The Instinct of Workman-
    ship. New York: MacMillan.
Walker, Charles R., ed. 1968. Technology, Industry,
    and Man: The Age of Acceleration. New York:
    McGraw-Hill.
Walker, Charles R., and Guest, Robert H. 1952. The
    Man on the Assembly Line. Cambridge, Mass.:
    Harvard University Press.
Warner, W. Lloyd, and Low, J. O. 1947. The Social
    System of the Modern Factory. Yankee City
    Series, Vol. IV. New Haven, Conn.: Yale
    University Press.
Watson, Bill. 1971. "Counter-Planning on the Shop
    Floor," Radical America. Vol. 5, n. 3.
Webb, Eugene J., Campbell, Donald T., Schwartz,
    Richard D., and Sechrist, Lee. 1966.
    Unobtrusive Measures. Chicago: Rand McNally.
Weber, Max. 1964. The Theory of Social and
    Economic Organization. T. Parsons, ed. New
    York: Free Press.
Whyte, William Foote. 1948. Human Relations in the
    Restaurant Industry. New York: McGraw-Hill.
Whyte, William Foote. 1961. Men at Work. Home-
    wood, Ill.: Dorsey Press.
Whyte, William Foote. 1969. Organizational
    Behavior: Theory and Application. Homewood,
    Ill.: Irwin-Dorsey.
Wilson, H. B. 1974. Democracy and the Workplace.
    Montreal: Black Rose
Woodward, Joan. 1965. Industrial Organization:
    Theory and Practice. New York: Oxford Uni-
    versity Press.